Retiring in America:

It's All About Income

Retiring in America:

It's All About Income

By Andy Barkate MS

Contents

Section IV – Putting It All Together

Foreword

I was an 18-year-old freshman in college when I took my first economics course. I wasn't sure why I was taking it or what economics was all about, but a classmate explained if I planned on majoring in business, economics was one of the requirements. So, off I went. It was a long time ago, but I remember it vividly. I can still hear the professor throwing out terms and phrases such as supply, demand, marginal utility and GNP. I felt as if I was in quicksand and remember wondering "what have I gotten myself into."

But a funny thing happened. Somewhere during that first semester of Economics 101, things started to click. I began understanding the relationships between economics and monetary policy and its effect on our lives.

The economist Percy L. Greaves said, "Economics is not a dry subject. It is not a dismal subject. It is not about statistics. It is about human life. It is about the ideas that motivate human beings. It is about how men act from birth until death. It is about the most important and interesting drama of all — human action." *and reaction*

For me, economics helped explain why things happened the way they did. It helped me understand why my mutual fund was going down in value, why interest rates were so high, why it was becoming hard to find a job and why prices kept rising (at that time, I was mainly concerned about the price of beer and pizza). *and dealer formula :)*

Since then, I've had a lifelong fixation on economics. I believe if more people had a strong working knowledge of economic principles, we'd be less apt to be misled by those who make the economic policies that affect our lives. ✒

After graduation I was fortunate to land a job at a major aircraft manufacturing company. My job title was engineer, but that was far from the truth. I spent much of my day looking at budgets and financial proposals. Three years later, I landed what I thought was my dream job, Dean Witter Reynolds, one of the major brokerage firms on Wall Street. I was a 24-year-old stockbroker; boy, I thought life was good. It didn't take me long to realize that "stockbroker" was a fancy title for a lot of very hard work. But I loved it.

To make a long story short, I spent the last 30 years in the financial services business and now own and manage my own financial and retirement planning firm. I've been fortunate enough over that time to work with literally thousands of individuals and small businesses designing, implementing and managing savings and retirement plans. I've not only continued to learn about finance, markets and investment strategies but have come to understand a great deal about people.

Back 30 years ago, when a person came into my office I thought it was because they wanted to invest their money in order to reap the big rewards the stock market offered. It took me a few years, but I came to realize most people didn't like to take big risks with their hard-earned savings. Most were hoping for a competitive return and above all... safety.

Retiring in America: It's All About Income is about seeing the world for what it is and understanding that the quality of our financial lives is up to us. We'll discuss the financial problems we currently face and important habits and methods we must use in order to thrive despite the unpredictable world we live in today.

Most economic events are out of our control as individuals, therefore we'll focus on retirement strategies that we can control. The probability of reaching your financial goals, whatever they may be, are more a function of you and your choices, not random incidents that you can't predict or control.

Dear reader, as you progress through this book you'll find a common theme of "income and lifestyle." It is my opinion that *income* is the main purpose of retirement planning. Said another way, sufficient income to maintain your lifestyle throughout retirement is the brass ring, the big enchilada or the Holy Grail of financial and retirement planning. Right?

If you were hoping I'd reveal the newest sure-fire way to beat the market or how to become a millionaire in three easy steps, Then I hate to inform you that buying this book was a waste of your money. If that's your goal, may I suggest buying a lottery ticket and saying a prayer?

A plan without action is a dream; action without a plan is a nightmare....
--Chinese proverb

It doesn't matter if you're 25 years old and just starting out or you've been retired for 10 years, if your goal is to build a retirement plan that will pay for your lifestyle, this book aims to give you the tools.

It's no secret we have formidable obstacles ahead of us. If asked, *what most worries you about your financial future,* many people will point to the massive swings in the stock market over the last decade. We all remember what the Tech Wreck and market collapse of 2000-2002 did, not to mention the mortgage crisis and Great Recession of 2007-09 and the hangover we continue to suffer through. Both events caused stock prices to drop over 40%, which made many retirees and soon-to-be retirees rethink their decisions.

But the stock market is only a symptom of what worries most retirees. In virtually every study and survey done over the last 20 years, retirees say their biggest fear isn't the stock market, it's running out of money!

As devastating as these events were, market volatility is but one of the concerns that can derail retirement plans. The glitz of the stock market gets the headlines, but it's the nagging details like inflation, longevity, debt and taxes that are the unsung and underappreciated killers of retirement dreams.

I've spoken to literally thousands of individuals preparing for retirement and I've never met one who retired without believing their income would be enough to pay their bills. But underestimating the importance of inflation, longevity, debt and taxes will eventually erode the lifestyle you desire.

Understanding how to control these retirement killers can be one of the most powerful weapons to help you live the
retirement lifestyle you've always dreamed of. Think about it. What do you want to do after you retire? Would you like to travel more, spend time with your grandchildren, create a few new hobbies or write the next Great American novel? The point is, whatever your dreams are, they'll in most cases take money. It may sound a bit shallow, but it's true.

I've always believed that any problem can be solved with a "plan." Creating a retirement lifestyle for yourself is no different. That's not to say your plan won't have detours, obstacles and headwinds because it will.

In this book, we'll discuss many of the obstacles facing retirees in the 21st century, as well as some of the mistakes and assumptions that can get in your way. I'll use a lot of ink discussing ways to create and maintain the lifeblood of any retirement plan.... income. And then we'll finish off by bringing it all together, showing you methods to structure your own retirement roadmap.

So, if you're ready..... Let's go.

A Note to the Reader

This book is intended to get you to look at retirement planning from a different angle, to get you to challenge the status quo and conventional wisdom of the financial establishment. This book is not intended to give you specific tax or investment advice. Additionally, it is not my intention to give you any personal recommendations whatsoever.

Choosing one or more of the retirement strategies outlined in this book should only be undertaken with consultation with a competent retirement planner or financial advisor. Each one of you has a unique financial situation and set of goals that should be considered prior to using any financial strategy, including the ones discussed in this book.

Also, as of the writing of this text, the retirement and financial strategies discussed are relevant. However, this does not mean that tax and/or legal changes will not alter or render them ineffective in the future. I encourage you to seek competent professional advice regarding the current relevance of tax and legal matters and their implications to your specific situation.

Lastly, open your mind and enjoy the read.....

The Problem

P lanning for secure retirement means you'll be hurdling a variety of challenges. Most that we'll discuss in this chapter shouldn't be foreign to you; however, failing to adequately consider these obstacles could put an otherwise sound retirement in peril. A mentor once told me a mistake with a small amount of money leads to a small loss, but a small mistake with a large amount of money is quite the opposite.

A Penny Saved Is a Penny Earned

The question isn't at what age I want to retire, it's at what income.
–George Foreman

To be blunt, as a country we're not saving nearly enough to properly fund our lifestyles in retirement. Many of you have read the statistics regarding retirement savings, but in order to make a point, they bear repeating.

According to the Retirement Benefit Research Institute, 46% of all Americans have less than $10,000 in retirement savings and 29% have less than $1,000.

Furthermore, according to the Pension Rights Center in Washington, D.C., of the 50 million Americans participating in 401(k) plans, the average balance is just over $60,000. Workers within 10 years of retirement have saved approximately $78,000 and one-third of them have less than $25,000. More shocking, over half of U.S. workers have no retirement plan at all.

With the number of private companies offering pension plans decreasing every year (in 2007, 21% of the privately held companies offered pension plans), more of the burden of funding retirement will fall squarely on our shoulders. The statistics mentioned above are certainly dire, but you might be asking yourself how much do I need to save and invest in order to fund my retirement and maintain my lifestyle?

Let's say you need $5,000 per month to pay your bills and fund your lifestyle. To keep it simple, let's leave taxes and inflation out of it for now. If you assume that your investments can average 5% a year and you need this income to last for 30 years, you'll need $935,000.

Now, if that didn't get your attention, let's be more realistic and add 3% inflation and pay the government 25% in taxes. Under the circumstances, your $935,000 nest egg would last you just about 17 years. That's perfectly okay if you plan on dying about 16 years after you retire.

It's apparent many Americans are sticking their head in the sand when it comes to saving for retirement. Perhaps they believe that Social Security will bail them out? Currently the average Social Security recipient receives $14,780 annually or around $22,000 for a couple. As you can see without substantial savings or other income sources, Social Security provides a meager existence.

Many Americans understand they're behind schedule, but it becomes easier to adopt the ostrich approach and stick their heads in the sand and hope the problem goes away. For others, making up for lost time means taking high levels of risk by investing a large percentage of retirement accounts in riskier asset classes, such as individual stocks and mutual funds. Unfortunately, taking on risk is a double-edged sword; it can either help or hurt you. Just ask anyone who's tried to maintain the value of their retirement account while navigating the markets over the last decade.

Taxes ... The Four-Letter Word

The income tax has made more liars out of the American people than golf has.

–Will Rogers

To many of us, 'taxes' is truly a four-letter word. Taxes are the price we pay for living in a country as great as America. Now having said that, the *price* seems to be rising all the time. Paying taxes is a major part of our financial lives. Just think about how investment returns are typically quoted.... I made 7%... after tax. Or my investment is expected to return 6%, after tax. Taxes are something we must constantly work to reduce.

From a retiree's point of view, taxes can be one of the largest expenses. Throughout our working lives, taxes are a nuisance, constantly nipping at our heels, absorbing money that could be used to fund our lifestyles as well as retirement.

At my firm we work with small businesses as well as individuals in preparing retirement plans. Over the years, I've had countless conversations with individuals and participants in company 401(k) plans regarding whether it's wiser to pay taxes now by using a Roth IRA or a Roth 401(k) or using the traditional methods of retirement planning that defers taxes until you actually spend your money.

Everyone, no matter what age, believes they're paying too much in taxes. When I'm talking to a 30 or 40 something-year-old, I make a point of saying that *"if you think you're paying too much in taxes now, just wait."* Think about it. Stereotypically, when you're younger, you're probably raising children and paying off a mortgage. Both of these activities provide wonderful tax deductions. As you age, your children tend to grow up and move away, and your mortgage hopefully is paid down. All this is happening when you're entering your peak earning years. In most cases you lose many of your tax deductions just when you need them. Now, picture yourself retired. Hopefully you're thinking of the solid income you'll have because you saved well and successfully paid off your debts. At the stage of your life where you want to enjoy living, taxes will be a constant companion.

Establishing income streams that will be tax advantaged to help you avoid the tax man and keep more of your money to spend on you, will be discussed in detail in Chapter 3.

Many of us bought into the idea that we should save money through our 401(k)s, IRAs, TSPs and other tax-qualified savings vehicles because when we retired our tax bracket would be lower than when we were working. That's supposed to mean we pay less taxes when we pull it out to spend it during retirement. This might turn out to be one of the biggest cons of all time. Isn't it funny how old ideas seem to linger on forever?

Not only are there fewer federal tax brackets than there were 20 years ago, but it's not unusual to retire and have your income decrease while remaining in the same tax bracket. Many current retirees are painfully experiencing this right now.

Will taxes increase in the future? This is the current debate going on in America. Whether taxes should go up or down isn't the point. What you should be concerned with is how will they affect you and what can you do about it.

If you ask any seasoned veteran in the tax or financial planning business about the future direction for income taxes, you'll likely hear the same response – they're going higher! And there appears to be legitimate justification for this belief. The chart on the opposite page shows the current federal income tax rates just put into effect early in 2013.

As you can see, the federal income tax rates get progressively larger as we make more money. This is no secret, but the bigger question is will they get more intrusive as time goes on? Consider the size of the federal budget, $3.7 trillion (that's 3.7 with 11 zeroes behind it) in 2012. The amount of total revenues from all sources of income was $2.6 billion, leaving us with a budget deficit of $1.1 billion (1,100,000,000,000). And this is just one year! If you do the quick math, we're spending almost 42% more than we're bringing in.

What's a trillion anyway?

This figure has been batted around indiscriminately for the past several years. Most people have a hard time visualizing how large a trillion really is; here's a mental picture that might help....

Let's say every $1 equals 1 second....
- 1 million seconds equals 13 days ago... I bet you can remember what you were doing then.
- 1 billion seconds was 31 years ago.... How's your memory?
- 1 trillion seconds was 31,688 years ago..... Get the picture?

Andy Barkate

Table: 2013 Tax Rates and Brackets		
Filing Status	Taxable Income	Rate
Single	$0 to $8,925*:	10%
	$8,925* to $36,250:	15%
	$36,250 to $87,850:	25%
	$87,850 to $183,250:	28%
	$183,250 to $398,350:	33%
	$398,350 to $400,000:	35%
	$400,000+:	39.6%
Joint	$0 to $17,850*:	10%
	$17,850* to $72,500:	15%
	$72,500 to $146,400:	25%
	$146,400 to $223,050:	28%
	$223,050 to $398,350:	33%
	$398,350 to $450,000:	35%
	$450,000+:	39.6%
Head of Household	$0 to $12,750*:	10%
	$12,750* to $48,600:	15%
	$48,600 to $125,450:	25%
	$125,450 to $203,150:	28%
	$203,150 to $398,350:	33%
	$398,350 to $425,000:	35%
	$425,000+:	39.6%

Our current national debt is over $17 trillion. In seconds, that's 538,696 years. The next time one of the talking heads in Washington or on Wall Street uses the word trillion, it should catch your attention.

Any rational-thinking individual can easily understand why our current fiscal condition isn't sustainable. Even if you take into consideration that the federal budget deficit is expected to fall a bit in 2013, the difference between the amount of money we spend as a country and the amount of money we generate in revenues creates a gaping hole.

Basically, the government can raise money in three ways.

- Tax it
- Borrow it
- Print it

When you consider these three avenues, perhaps you'll scratch your head just as I do because they all can have negative economic consequences, if not handled in a responsible manner. So you must ask yourself, if the government is spending more money than it's bringing in, where will they come up with the rest? The likely answer is raising taxes. You may think the answer is to reduce government spending, but then you assume that Washington operates in the *real world* as you and I do... They don't.

Ronald Reagan once said, "The thing nearest to eternal life ever seen on this earth is a government program."

Throughout 2011-2013, we've witnessed countless stalemates, deadlines and debates emanating from Washington, all regarding how to best fund our country's budget. Taxes and spending have been at the center of these debates. If the compromise reached at the end of 2012 is any indication of what we can expect in the future, hold onto your wallet because higher taxes will most likely be the answer coming from our lawmakers in the future.

Let's take it a bit further. If taxes do increase in the future, who are the ones most likely to be targeted? Well, the fact you're reading this book most likely puts you in the crosshairs. If you are responsible enough to understand that you must build, maintain and protect your retirement assets, this probably means you're earning a level of income that puts the bull's eye squarely on you.

Consider the breakdown on Figure 2. It's a bit of an *eye-opener*, isn't it, with all the rhetoric surrounding the movement to increase taxes on the top 5% of income earners, you know *"the fat cats."* The next time you look in the mirror, you just might see one of those fat cats because as the chart indicates, if your adjusted gross income or AGI is a bit above $150,000 annually, you fit the definition.

I work with individuals and business owners every day, and it's not uncommon to have a husband and wife sitting at my desk with an income above the $150,000 mark. You may be a teacher, engineer, a civil servant or small business owner, and between you and your spouse, you're rich, at least in the eyes of the federal government.

Let's use a bit of intuitive reasoning. As you can see in the chart below, if you're in the top 5% of the income earners you're already paying almost 59% of the total federal income tax. So you may think to yourself, *"I'm already paying my share."*

However, lawmakers don't see it that way; in their eyes it's fair to have you pay more because you can afford to. I understand that fairness is a relative term. It's fair to the one who receives government subsidies or entitlements, but it may not seem fair to those who pay for those government programs.

Another rationale for the increased tax burden heaped on top wage earners is the fact that it's *politically safe* for those in Washington. Consider if you're in the top 10% of wage earners, this means the other 90% of the wage earners make less. Therefore, if Washington aims a tax increase at the top 10%, the other 90% will be unaffected, how you do think that piece of legislation will turn out? If individuals have the opportunity to cast votes to maintain a government program that benefits them and have someone else pay for it.... how do you think they'll vote?

Don't get me wrong I'm not bashing the American form of government. In fact, I believe we still have one of the best government models on earth. But that doesn't mean it doesn't have its share of challenges.

Figure 2

Who Pays Federal Income Taxes

Percentiles Ranked by AGI	AGI Threshold on Percentiles	Percentage of Federal Personal Income Tax Paid
Top 1%	$343,927	36.73
Top 5%	$154,643	58.66
Top 10%	$112,124	70.47
Top 25%	$66,193	87.30
Top 50%	$32,396	97.75
Bottom 50%	<$32,396	2.25

Note: AGI is Adjusted Gross Income
Source: Internal Revenue Service

Source: National Taxpayers Union, 2009

It's not my aim to make political statements when I talk about income taxes; I'm attempting to show things for what they really are. We are currently in an environment of big government, and it has a voracious need for income. It's a pretty good bet that a large part of the necessary income will be generated from higher taxes. Therefore, the retirement-minded investor needs to employ strategies and methods to lessen their tax burden. We'll discuss many of these strategies and methods in detail in Chapter 3.

Inflation...... The Silent Killer

Inflation is as violent as a mugger, as frightening as an armed robber and as deadly as a hit man.

–Ronald Reagan

When you consider that most of us will be retired for approximately 20 to 30 years, not only must we have income and assets to last that long, but one must analyze how the purchasing power of this income will be affected by inflation. When I speak publicly to a group of individual investors, to make my point about inflation I look around the room to gauge the approximate ages of the audience and then ask, *"How many of you paid more for your last car than you did for your first house?"* The response is always the same, there's a pregnant pause and then a few chuckles and then hands start going up. Think about it. How much did last year's vacation cost? Now consider the cost of the vacation you took 10 years ago. Think about what a vacation might cost 10 years from now, and you'll get my point.

Another way to bring inflation into reality is to look at nominal and inflation-adjusted stock market performance. As the chart on the next page indicates, the stock market (Dow Jones) increased dramatically over the hundred years between 1900 and 2000.

The index was valued at 68 in 1900 and rose to 11,500 just 100 years later. But when adjusted for inflation, the stock market's performance doesn't seem near as dramatic; 11,500 becomes approximately 450.

Most retirees live on a fixed income. Inflation can, over time, wreak havoc on the lifestyle of a family on a fixed income. Don't fall into the trap of believing that because Social Security is indexed for inflation as well as your government pension (private pensions are typically not indexed for inflation) that the effects of inflation won't squeeze you. You must try to see the forest through the trees.

Consider how the government calculates the annual increases on Social Security and pensions. The CPI-W (Consumer Price Index for Urban Wage Earners and Clerical Workers) is used to calculate annual increases. In 2012, the CPI-W increased by 1.7%, therefore Social Security and pension incomes increased by the same amount in 2013. That may sound well and good until you consider the effect inflation has on your current expenditures. How you spend your money plays a large part in determining how inflation will affect you. Consider the 2013 inflation forecasts for some of the spending categories we'll spend our money on.

- According to the US Department of Agriculture, food prices will go up approximately 3.5%.
- If you're sending your child to college, costs are expected to rise 4.8% next year, according to College Board.
- Price Waterhouse Coopers experts believe health insurance costs will rise 7.5% in 2013.

THE REAL DOW

Adjusted for consumer-price inflation, the Dow Jones Industrial Average has risen less, and performed differently, than the nominal Dow used in most charts.

(Chart relfects monthly data)

NOMINAL DJIA

INFLATION-ADJUSTED DJIA

15000
12500
10000
7500

5000

2500

1000

500

100

10

1900's   20's   40's   60's   80's   00's

Note: Based on Dow's value in 1900. Chart is logarithmic, with vertical scale compressed to show changes in percentage terms. A rise from 100 to 110 takes the same space as a rise from 1000 to 1100, since both are 10% changes.
Source: Ned Davis Research

The one bright spot is most energy categories are not expected to increase by much. According to the U.S. Energy Information Administration, gasoline prices will be flat but natural gas prices and heating oil prices will rise approximately 2.5%.

As you can see, many of the categories the average American spends a large portion of their monthly income on are increasing at a rate much faster than the CPI-W will increase your Social Security and pension. Eventually, something's gotta give, and unfortunately in many cases it's lifestyle.

I have seen this firsthand. I've been in the retirement planning business almost 30 years, and therefore many clients of my firm have been with us for 20 years-plus. What started out to be a very comfortable retirement lifestyle has over time been endangered by the long-term effects of inflation, not to mention the unexpected expenses life sometimes throws at us.

Here's a basic example. Let's say you plan on retiring tomorrow, and you think you need $5000 a month to maintain your lifestyle. In just a little over 20 years, you'll need about $9,000 a month if inflation would average 3% (historical average is 3.01%) and that's just to continue the same spending habits that you have now. Wow.....

If inflation averaged 4%, you would need approximately $11,000 over 20 years; if it averaged 5%, you would need about $13,250. Get the message? You might think inflation won't bother you because you won't live 20 years after you retire. Think again. According to life insurance actuarial tables, the average 65-year-old married couple has a pretty good chance of at least one spouse living to the mid-90s.

Where will inflation go from here?

The truth is, no one knows for sure. But if history is any guide the rapid increase in money supply we've experienced in the past several years will lead to elevated inflation levels. It's no secret since the recent mortgage and financial crisis our government and Federal Reserve have aggressively increased the monetary base (money supply). This is being done in an effort to rekindle U.S. economic activity, but, if successful, there may be very damaging side effects, mainly inflation and devaluation of the U.S. dollar. The chart below depicts the growth in money supply we've experienced over the past few years.

Figure 3

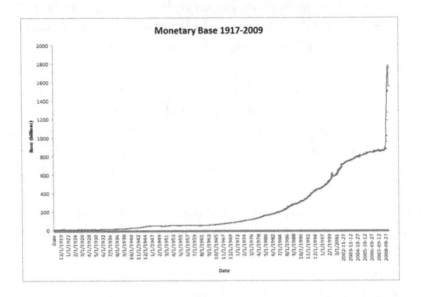

In basic economics, AD=AS (Aggregate Demand equals Aggregate Supply). In terms of the money supply, if increased by 4%, you'd expect aggregate demand to increase by 4% because there is more currency in circulation in which to consume goods and services. If AS and AD both increase to 4%, there will be no inflation. In other words, if the money supply grows at the same rate as real economic output, the result would be stable prices or the absence of inflation. However, if the money supply grows faster than real economic output, by definition we're bound to have inflation.

So clearly, we've had a rapid increase in money supply over the last few years, but we've had a very subdued level of inflation. How is this possible?

Keynesian economists will explain it as the "liquidity trap." When the economy is suffering through a recession, an increase to the money supply helps get underutilized resources deployed. In other words, because the economy is operating at a slower pace than is optimal, it's got room to grow and expand before things start to tighten up. In this condition, economists will argue that money supply can grow much faster than economic output and not cause inflation.

In the Keynesian "liquidity trap," interest rates can fall to extremely low levels and people will still opt to hold onto their money in lieu of spending it in the economy. Therefore, the increase in money supply does not actually reach the economy.

Does this sound familiar? Many economists will argue that this situation is happening today. We've experienced a rapid increase in the money supply as noted above, but our economic growth has been very modest. Under normal circumstances, this is inflationary. However, the vast majority of new currency in circulation has not reached the economy to act as fuel for consumption; it's being held in banks and financial institutions. This economic phenomenon has occurred during past economic downturns in the U.S.

When the economic output starts to increase, there's a high probability this pent-up money supply will find its way into the economy and cause inflation. The question is, will we have a normal cyclical bout of inflation or will it resemble what we experienced in the '70s and early '80s?

It's safe to say inflation will be a fact that investors and retirees will have to deal with for a long time.

Longevity...

It's not surprising people are living longer now than any other time in history. Hallmark is producing birthday cards for those who reach 100. Longevity comes with a greater opportunity to experience more of life and its blessings, but it also comes with its share of concerns such as health-care costs and sufficient income.

A *Wall Street Journal* article in October 2006 titled *"An Age Old Problem: How to Make Sure Your Money Lasts As Long As You Do"* discussed this issue at length. The article stated that a 65-year-old married couple has a 68% chance of at least one of them living to age 85 and 42% chance of one of them living to age 90.

Think about the people you know. How many are currently in their 70s and 80s? Many of our clients are in this age group, and I'm constantly surprised by their energy and vitality. It constantly reminds me of how bright our future is when it comes to enjoying retirement and aging with dignity.

Another unfortunate fact of life is that health-care costs will be a constant financial burden. The Bureau of Labor Statistics estimates that in 2012, health-care costs increased by 4%, roughly twice the inflation rate of the economy in general. Moreover, a recent Fidelity Investments survey concluded that the average retired couple will spend approximately $240,000 in *out-of-pocket costs* to pay for healthcare during their retired lives.

The fact that people are living longer makes thoughtful planning essential to ensure quality of life can be maintained as we age and also provide us the confidence in knowing the uncertainties of health will not cause financial hardship.

The Stock Market Will Take Care of Me

Over the past 30 years, we've seen some of the best and worst market cycles in history. For those between the ages of 50 and 70, our first real foray into the stock market was in the 1980s. Remember the good old days when the markets seem to go up forever? Between 1984 and 2000, the Dow Jones Industrial Average increased roughly 1000%, the longest and steepest bull market in history. The positive take-away from this is obvious...we all made money. However, the downside is we came to believe this is just what the market does... it goes up. We were seduced into a false sense of security by a 16-year-long bull market.

Many investors started to believe they had figured out the market, and Wall Street was happy to let them believe it. I can remember in the late '90s viewing a TV commercial produced by one of the major Wall Street firms. The commercial depicted several young housewives sitting around the coffee table watching their toddlers play. The conversation wasn't about their children, but about how easy it was to set up an online trading account and buy stocks. The implication was *it was child's play*. It wasn't too much longer before the dot.com bubble burst and economic reality set in.

14

The graph on the next page depicts a 115-year history of the Dow Jones Industrial Average. During this period, there have been four *Secular Bull Market* periods where the market increased dramatically (green) and four *Secular Bear Market* periods where the market lost value or traded sideways (red). It seems obvious that you'd want to be in the market as rises up and parked on the sidelines during declines. We all know that's easy to say but difficult, if not impossible, to do.

As the chart on the next page clearly shows, the market tends to have relatively long cycles where stock prices increase and sometimes abrupt and long cycles of price decline or trade sideways (Secular Bull & Bear Markets). The question you must ask yourself is where are we now? Is the market poised for another increase or will we continue to trade sideways, or possibly enter a new bear market? This is an important question because your money is at stake.

If you picked up your phone tomorrow and called 10 stockbrokers or investment companies to ask those questions, what do you think their answers would be? Do you think they have a vested interest in implying that the market's future is bright? I'm not saying individuals who work for investment companies are bad people; they're not. But you must understand that you're asking advice from a person whose livelihood depends on your belief in their product (the stock market).

The facts are that no one knows from day to day, week to week or year to year where the stock market is headed. The stock market can be an excellent long-term investment, but you must consider the risk it possesses. In the end, you're the one taking the risk, you're the one whose money is on the line, and you're the one who will have to make the tough financial decisions if your retirement nest egg is damaged by a bear market. Neither your stockbroker nor the company he or she works for are taking any risks.... It's just you.

Figure 4

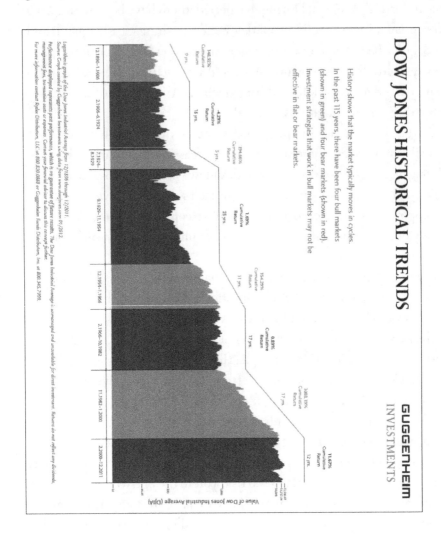

Risk Shifting

When you're invested directly in the financial markets, you're the one taking all the risk. The retirement accounts of most Americans are comprised primarily of stocks, bonds and mutual funds. While these areas have proven to be a valid way to grow retirement savings, they also carry the risk of price fluctuations that can cause *account spend down* when these assets are used to supply income. We'll discuss this more in Chapters 2 and 3.

It's not a new concept to attempt to reduce the risk of your retirement accounts the closer you get to your target retirement age. But the act of reducing risk still implies that your retirement accounts carry some level of risk. Doesn't it make sense to shift as much risk away from your assets and transfer it (risk) to someone else?

Here's an example. Ask yourself why you buy automobile insurance? Does owning this type of insurance protect you from future automobile accidents? Of course not, but it does shift the financial risk associated with an automobile accident from you back to the insurance company. If you're involved in an accident, the automobile repairs as well as potential medical expenses and property damage are liabilities of your insurance company. If you didn't own this type of insurance, guess who's on the hook to pay for the damages. In effect, you're shifting potential financial risk from you to a third party. Other types of insurance work the same way, such as life insurance, medical insurance, homeowners insurance and disability insurance.

When you buy insurance, you're effectively "shifting risk."

While owning insurance can't prevent bad things from happening, shifting the financial liability protects you and your family as well as your assets.

If you're reading this book, you're obviously concerned about your retirement. Therefore, it's probably safe to say you understand the value of purchasing insurance in order to protect against life's unforeseen calamities.

So, if it makes sense to insure the things that are important to you, doesn't it also make sense to insure your retirement accounts?

This concept might be foreign to many of you reading this book. You may think the only way to protect yourself against financial market's unpredictable nature is to "hold your nose" and invest in low yielding fixed accounts such as CDs and money market accounts.

Most investors believe they must perform a balancing act when investing their money. They must somehow find the perfect equilibrium between the risk and potential higher returns of the stock market and the safety and low yields of fixed-income investment areas.

I am a big believer in "risk shifting." The more risk you can shift away from your retirement portfolio back to the investment company, the safer you'll be. I'll discuss methods that you can use in order to effectively shift risk and still reap the potential awards the financial markets offer. More about this in Chapter 3.

It will become apparent throughout reading *"Retiring in America – It's All About Income"* that I tend to be conservative when it comes to retirement planning. I've always believed retirement is a time to enjoy life, free from the stresses that come with the workplace and raising children. It should be a time we can enjoy our families, travel, give back to our communities or engage in the hobbies we never had time for in the past. And if prepared for properly, it can be a time void of the fear and trepidation that comes with financial worry.

This can be done.... But it will not be done by accident; it will take wisdom, aversion to following the crowd and the ability to look past the obvious.

My goal in this book is to discuss the concerns many investors have regarding maintaining their lifestyles throughout retirement and introduce concepts and methods that can bring more safety, stability and peace of mind.

Killing the
Sacred Cows

Many axioms and assumed truths can cause more harm than good. A few hundred years ago, the world was flat, about 100 years ago only birds flew and a couple of decades ago, if Steve Jobs had listened to every executive at major computer companies, we still might not have the personal computer.

Investing money has its own set of "sacred cows" that have been perpetuated by both the financial services industry and the financial media. To be successful when investing your retirement dollars, you must recognize them for what they are: outdated or simply untrue. The fact that you're reading this book means you're probably at the age when your money is too important to leave to chance. You've probably figured out that no matter who's giving you advice, you're the one taking the risks. Many of these axioms are designed to entice and placate you into keeping your money invested in risky assets at a time when it's not in your best interest to do so.

In this chapter, we'll discuss several of the sacred cows of investing that you need to be aware of in order to successfully avoid them. Here goes.....

Buy-and-Hold

I just made a killing in the stock market -- I shot my broker.

–Henny Youngman

For years the professional investment community has consistently sold "Buy-and-Hold" as the sure way to *win* in the stock market. All you had to do was pick a quality company stock or mutual fund, buy it and let the stock market and capitalism take its natural course. It didn't matter if it went down, if you held it long enough, it would come back up and lo and behold, you'll make money.

Many now call it "Buy-and-Pray."

What those on Wall Street failed to understand was that, in order for this philosophy to work, you needed to actually know a bit about which companies and mutual funds to buy and which ones to steer clear of, not to mention having a good idea of the general direction of the stock market is important. The old saying *"a rising tide raises all boats"* is generally true when it comes to stocks. In an increasing market cycle, approximately 80% of all stocks will rise. Both quality stocks and not so quality stocks (dogs) will all be pulled higher by a bull market. On the other hand, in a bear market both quality companies and weak companies will indiscriminately sell off. So it's far from being as simple as "buy-and-hold."

If you'd like just a little bit of proof, look at Figure 4 in Chapter 1. This offers clear evidence that the stock market has definable, long-term cycles. Buy-and-hold would have worked well if you decided to buy sometime in the '80s and early to mid- '90s, which just so happens to be the longest bull market in stock market history. It wouldn't work as well if you decided to buy in the late '90s.

If you don't believe me, a *Forbes* article published in July 2010, titled *"Buy-And-Hold Is Dead and Gone"* by author Sy Harding, sums it up very well when he said:

> *"Proof of the fallacy of buy-and-hold as a strategy is easy enough to find. In the 1929 crash and its aftermath the market lost 86% of its value and did not get back to its 1929 level until 1955, twenty-six years later. That was 26 years of waiting for buy and hold investors (if there still were any) for the market to 'come back.'*
>
> *"In 1965, just 11 years later, when the Dow reached 1,000 for the first time, the long 1965-1982 secular bear market began. For the next 17 years the Dow cycled between cyclical bull markets and cyclical bear markets, but did not manage to rise above its level of 1965 until late in 1982 (Figure 5). It was another 17 years in which buy and hold investors (again if there were any left) waited for the market to come back. Seventeen years of whipsawing heartbreak for buy and hold investors, but wonderful opportunities for market-timing."*

"That made a total of 41 of the 53 years between 1929 and 1982 that buy and hold investors were waiting and hoping for the market to get back to previous levels."

Figure 5

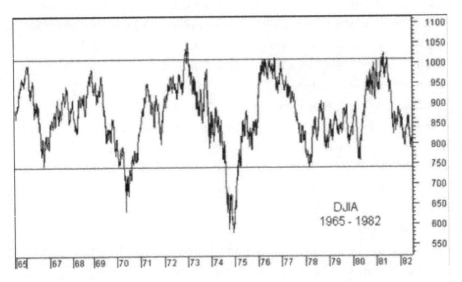

DJIA
1965 - 1982

You might be thinking, "If I pick the right stocks it will all work out." While that is true, it's much easier said than done. Let's look at a couple of examples from well-known and widely held companies.

If you bought Apple computer in February 2002, you'd have paid about $7.50 per share; 10 years later it was worth around $450 per share, reaching a high of $667 in September 2012. If you bought this company 10 years ago, congratulations! You hit one of the biggest home runs in the stock market's history. But what if, like countless other investors, you were sucked in during Apple's phenomenal run in 2012? There is a good chance you'd be losing money holding the stock that made Wall Street history.

Let's look at something a bit more mundane. General Electric is arguably one of the best-run companies in the world. If you'd bought GE in early 2003, you'd paid proximally $25.50 per share; 10 years later, it was worth approximately $23. During the mortgage meltdown of 2008-09, GE fell to $10 per share. I wonder how many investors were scared by headlines and subsequently bailed out of the stock thinking it might get worse.

It pays to remember that every investor selling shares of stock is convinced it's not worth holding, while that same stock is being bought by someone who thinks exactly the opposite.

Don't think it could really happen? Ask the average Japanese investor....

Remember back in the 1980s, when Japan's economy and stock market were considered a juggernaut? On December 29, 1989, the Japanese stock market (Nikkei) hit its all-time high of 38,915.87. Today, almost 24 years later, the Nikkei stands at 13,615.19 or 65% below its high (see Nikkei Graph 1985-2013).

The reason I cite the Japanese economy is that in the 1980s, the lack of prudent economic and fiscal policy exerted by the Japanese government allowed their economy and stock markets to create unsustainable price levels, which, as we all know now, failed.

Figure 6: *Nikkei Graph 1985-2013*

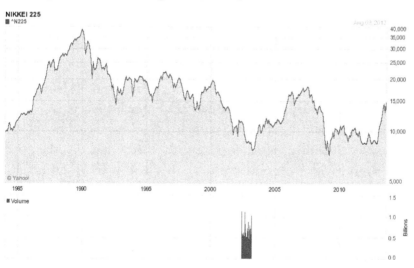

Currently, is the U.S. government engaging in risky economic policy in order to help revitalize our economy after the 2008–2009 market correction and great recession? Many economists and market strategist argue that there are striking similarities to what happened in Japan.

Over the long run, I'm sure the Japanese stock market will eventually reach and exceed its 1989 highs. But as the famous English economist John Maynard Keynes once said, *"Over the long run, we're all dead."*

The important question is: *Can I afford the risk and uncertainty?*

Now, do you think the average Japanese stockholder believes in the buy-and-hold strategy? If you were a Japanese investor relying on the stock market to provide a comfortable retirement, what do you think you're doing now? Who's picking up the slack in their retirement plans caused by the two-decade-long bear market?

Now ask yourself: *If something similar to Japan happens here, can I afford to cross my fingers and hope that the buy-and-hold strategy works?*

4% Income Rule

Since the mortgage meltdown and subsequent stock market decline of 2008-09, the 4% rule has been getting a lot of attention. Devised in the early 1990s by financial planner William Bergen, the 4% this rule attempts to quantify the amount of income (inflation adjusted) that can be withdrawn from an investment portfolio of stocks and bonds without running dry over a 30-year period (the assumed length of retirement). Mr. Bergen concluded that an allocation of 60% U.S. stocks and 40% bonds is the optimal mix to produce the highest level of sustainable income.

By using this method of producing retirement income, the odds are relatively low you'll outlive your money, or so the theory goes. In other words, if you retire with $500,000 in your 401(k), TSP or IRA, how much could you withdraw annually and be reasonably assured you're not going to run out of money?

Generally, analysts and economists attempted to understand how much income a portfolio consisting of different asset classes (mainly stocks and bonds) could generate over an extended period of time without being exhausted. Most academics studying this dilemma concluded that 4% was a safe withdrawal rate. For many years the financial planning community used this research as the unquestioned truth of the amount of income to advise their clients to withdraw from their retirement accounts.

You may be thinking to yourself, wait a minute, I've heard for years that the average rate of return of the stock market is somewhere around 9%. So why then, are you telling me that I must only take out 4%?

Herein lies one of the biggest misconceptions within the financial planning community. While it's true the stock market over the last half-century averaged around 9%, this average return has nothing to do with how much money you can safely take out of your portfolio on an annual basis, as discussed in the 4% rule.

You see, there are typically two phases of a retirement account: *accumulation and distribution.* During the accumulation phase, you're adding money to your retirement account and as the market ebbs and flows over time, you're effectively practicing "dollar-cost averaging" or DCA. As the market declines, the contributions you're adding to your retirement plan effectively buy more shares, which amplify the gains during an increasing market.

The distribution phase (retirement) can do just the opposite. When you take distribution in the form of income from your retirement account "reverse dollar-cost averaging" or RDCA is a result. It works like this. Say you take out $1,000 a month from your retirement account. Each month assets (shares of stocks bonds or mutual funds) must be sold in order to accommodate the monthly distribution. As share prices fall in a declining market, additional shares must be sold in order to provide the same $1,000 distribution. You may be thinking that it would work just the opposite in an increasing market... That sounds reasonable, but the math doesn't work out that way.

During your retirement years (distribution or income phase), the average rate of return of your retirement account means very little. It's the *sequence of the returns* that is paramount. Figure 7 illustrates this. In this example, we have two retirees, Mr. Smith and Ms. Jones. They're both retiring with $100,000 and they're distributing $5,000 annually. The average rate of return of their retirement portfolio over 30 years is exactly the same: 4.5%. So why then does Mr. Smith run out of money in year 17 and Ms. Jones have money to spare? The only thing that varies in these two examples is the *order* of annual return; remember, both retirement accounts average 4.5%. If you look closer you'll see that the orders of annual returns are exactly the opposite. In Mr. Smith's reality, the market fell the first few years he retired. Ms. Jones, however, had better luck. She happened to retire when the market was increasing.

Figure 7

	Mr. Smith		Ms. Jones	
	Sequence of returns (weak, then strong)	Balance	Sequence of returns (strong then weak)	Balance
Year 1	-5.30%	$89,700	11.90%	$106,900
Year 2	-2.10%	$82,816	8.90%	$111,414
Year 3	-7.30%	$71,771	11.50%	$119,227
Year 4	-11.20%	$58,732	9.90%	$126,030
Year 5	9.20%	$59,136	7.40%	$130,356
Year 6	2.70%	$55,732	9.80%	$138,131
Year 7	3.60%	$52,739	11.90%	$149,569
Year 8	-9.80%	$42,570	8.90%	$157,881
Year 9	-2.00%	$36,719	11.80%	$171,511
Year 10	10.20%	$34,464	10.20%	$184,005
Year 11	6.90%	$32,911	9.00%	$195,565
Year 12	-1.50%	$27,418	11.50%	$213,055
Year 13	2.10%	$22,993	9.20%	$227,656
Year 14	2.40%	$18,545	6.04%	$236,406
Year 15	9.20%	$15,251	-2.50%	$225,496
Year 16	-2.50%	$9,870	9.20%	$241,242
Year 17	6.04%	$5,466	2.40%	$242,032
Year 18	9.20%	$969	2.10%	$242,114
Year 19	11.50%	$0	-1.50%	$233,483
Year 20	9.00%	$0	6.90%	$244,593
Year 21	10.20%	$0	10.20%	$264,541
Year 22	11.80%	$0	-2.00%	$254,251
Year 23	8.90%	$0	-9.80%	$224,334
Year 24	11.90%	$0	3.60%	$227,410
Year 25	9.80%	$0	2.70%	$228,550
Year 26	7.40%	$0	9.20%	$244,577
Year 27	9.90%	$0	-11.20%	$212,184
Year 28	11.50%	$0	-7.30%	$191,695
Year 29	8.90%	$0	-2.10%	$182,669
Year 30	11.90%	$0	-5.30%	$167,988

You may be scratching your head wondering, "How can I make sure that I retire when the market is going up?" Obviously the answer is.... You can't! This is why the rationale underlying the 4% rule is important to understand.

To further explain the effects the sequence of returns has on your retirement account's value, consider the example in Figure 8. In this figure, we have two co-workers, Bob and Bill. Both had $500,000 in a 401(k) plan and will take income of $30,000 per year upon retirement. The only difference between these two is the *date* they retire. Bob retired in 1990 and Bill retired in 2000. As you can see, because of the yearly returns (Dow Jones Industrial Average), their account balances at the end of the decade differ drastically.

Successfully preventing your retirement accounts from depleting is not only dependent upon the amount of money you take from your accounts as income, but the variance in the returns achieved on those accounts, over time. Unfortunately, as a retiree you can't either control or predict the future returns your retirement account will receive when your money is invested in asset classes that fluctuate in value.

Figure 8

Bob: retired in 1990   Bill: retired in 2000

Year	Return	WD	Balance	Year	Return	WD	Balance
1990	-4.34%	$30,000	$449,602	2000	-6.18%	$30,000	$440,954
1991	20.32%	$30,000	$504,865	2001	-7.10%	$30,000	$381,776
1992	4.17%	$30,000	$494,667	2002	-16.76%	$30,000	$292,819
1993	13.72%	$30,000	$528,419	2003	25.32%	$30,000	$329,364
1994	2.14%	$30,000	509,085	2004	3.15%	$30,000	$308,794
1995	33.45%	$30,000	$639,340	2005	-0.61%	$30,000	$277,094
1996	26.01%	$30,000	$767,829	2006	16.29%	$30,000	$287,345
1997	22.64%	$30,000	$904,873	2007	6.43%	$30,000	$273,892
1998	16.10%	$30,000	$1,015,728	2008	-33.84%	$30,000	$161,359
1999	25.22%	$30,000	$1,234,328	2009	18.82%	$30,000	$156,081

As Figures 7 and 8 illustrate, relying on assets that change in value as the income source of your retirement account comes with more risk than most retirees realize. It's imperative that retirement accounts generate a predictable and sustainable return so they can produce long-term income in order to maintain your standard of living throughout retirement. We'll discuss strategies and techniques to provide sustainable income in Chapter 3.

So when should you start the transition from the accumulation phase to the distribution phase? The answer to this varies, but I believe the transition should start at least five years prior to retirement. Think back to the market correction of 2000-2002 and the more recent decline of 2008-2009. If you were planning to retire close to those dates and waited until you actually retired to transition or reallocate your retirement accounts into areas that would be less prone to market volatility..... you might still be working!

The 4% rule has come under increasing scrutiny. Low interest rates coupled with a volatile stock market caused many researchers to decrease the percentage withdrawal they believe safe. In the February 8, 2013, *MarketWatch* article "Retirements 4% Rule Gets Downsized," the author discussed the paradox of income, longevity and market risk as presented by the 4% rule. The author summed it up well stating, "*In today's markets, retirees who want a 90% probability of achieving their retirement income goal with a 30 year time horizon and 40% equity portfolio, should withdraw just 2.8%.*"

If her conclusion is correct, current and future retirees have much to think about. Do you reduce your lifestyle to meet your income or plan on working a bit longer in order to save more?

Let me be clear on something: *I don't hate the stock market.* If I did, it would be hypocritical because I own stocks and mutual funds within my retirement accounts. The point I'm trying to get across is that both history and research indicated assets that tend to fluctuate in value such as stocks, bonds and mutual funds are poor investment choices when solely being used to provide long-term, stable income.

Bonds Are a Safe Port in the Storm

As investors, we've been told bonds in our portfolios are a diversification tool that controls risk. While it's true that bonds are much less volatile than stocks, many investors are unaware that bonds also come with their own risks. Bonds have two basic levels of risk: credit risk and interest rate risk.

At their core, bonds are income instruments. When you're buying a bond, you're acting like a banker in that your lending money to a public company, state government or the federal government (the issuer). The issuer, in turn, promises to pay you a fixed interest rate for a set period of years, at which time your principal will be returned.

The credit risk of a bond is defined as the ability of the issuer to pay the ongoing interest payments as well as return the principal upon maturity. Credit risk is important to gauge when buying a bond from the public company or perhaps a state government or one of the entities within a state government. The federal government is assumed to be risk-free, therefore it carries no credit risk. I understand that because of recent federal budget deficits and the escalating national debt, many believe U.S. government bonds are not as risk-free as they used to be. But, for the purposes of this discussion I will assume that the U.S. government will not default on their obligations. They can always print more money, right?!

My goal in this section is to discuss interest rate risk and how it affects the market value of the bonds you may be holding.

As most know, interest rates and bond prices have an inverse relationship. As interest rates in the economy fall, bond prices push higher, and vice versa, when interest rates increase bond prices decline.

Here's a basic example. I purchase a $1,000 bond yielding 6% and maturing in 10 years. The issuer of this bond will pay me $60 a year for 10 years and then return my $1,000 investment. Now let's assume that sometime after my purchase, interest rates increase to 8%.

In this case, I own a bond that is only paying 6% when other similar bonds may be purchased at the new, higher interest rate. The market price of my bond will decline to a level at which the $60 annual interest yield will equal the current market interest rate (8%). The current value of my bond will be $750.

$60/.08= $750.

Of course, the opposite is true when interest rates decline. Let's say interest rates fall to 4%, my bond becomes more valuable because the $60 annual yield is greater than the amount a similar bond will currently provide. My bond will increase from its purchase price of $1,000 to approximately $1500.

$60/.04= $1500

It's not that simple, of course, because when it comes to the market nothing ever is! The bond's credit rating, maturity and duration also play into its market value.

The concept I'm trying to help you understand is that interest rate movements can have profound effects on the value of the bonds you hold. For those of you who'd like a detailed understanding of how bonds are priced, here you go.

$$\text{Bond Price} = \frac{C}{(1+i)} + \frac{C}{(1+i)^2} + \dots + \frac{C}{(1+i)^n} + \frac{M}{(1+i)^n}$$

Why is this important to understand now?

Currently, interest rates are at a level that most of us just a few years ago would not have imagined. Because of the housing and mortgage fiasco of 2007 and the subsequent stock market and economic decline that shortly followed, the U.S. Federal Reserve has adopted a low interest rate policy. By working hand in glove with the U.S. Treasury, the Federal Reserve injected trillions of dollars into our economy. This is being done in an effort to revitalize the economy and help it dig its way out of the deep recession that resulted from the unwinding of the housing and mortgage bubble.

Is there a new bubble forming?

Is the low interest rate environment we're in currently creating a bubble in the price of bonds? As the stock market plummeted in 2008-

2009, large sums of money were pulled from the stock market and subsequently placed in bonds. This is a classic "flight to safety" trade. Historically, in times of stock market decline investors will naturally move assets into safer areas such as bonds and money market accounts. While this makes sense, the astute investor must examine the probable outcomes of this strategy.

As the demand for safer asset classes such as bonds increases, the prices will naturally rise causing their effective yields to decline.

This phenomenon is highlighted in the October 18, 2012, *Business Week* article "Bond Fund Investors Beware."

Authors Saumya Vaishampayan and Margaret Collins discussed that from January through August 2008, U.S. investors poured $982 billion into bond funds while pulling $439 billion from stock funds. This trend continued and only recently is showing signs of stabilizing.

As a result of this mass exodus from stocks to bonds, the risk-averse investor has relied heavily on the stability of bonds. Over the past few years, they have been rewarded for their caution. The investors who were frightened out of stocks and fled to bonds in 2008 and 2009 were rewarded as interest rates declined and bond prices increased. From 2010 through 2012, interest rates consistently stayed at a remarkably low level, and in early 2013 the 10-year Treasury bill traded at approximately 1.9%. This recent stability may satisfy investors, but dangers lurk just around the corner.

The current generational low level of interest rates will not last forever. Invariably, rates will rise, causing bond prices to fall.

If you think about it, the "real return" of the 10-year Treasury bill is approximately 0%. Currently, inflation is averaging around 2% annually. If T-bills pay 1.9%, after inflation is considered your buying power hasn't increased a bit. The "real return" is the interest rate adjusted for the rate of inflation, which tells if you gained or lost ground.

And we haven't even considered taxes...

Rising interest rates are caused by any number of sources. The Federal Reserve's increase in the money supply may cause inflation as discussed in Chapter 1, or the U.S. economy may finally turned the corner and start to grow at a more rapid pace. In either case interest rates will likely increase from the current levels.

You may think, "If interest rates start to rise, I'll have time to simply move my money out of bonds and avoid the decline." While this is certainly possible, it is the same mindset many investors had before the 2008 and 2009 stock market decline. It's much easier said than done.

At the current low level of interest rates, as little as a 1% increase in the market rate of interest could cause bond prices to drop 15% or more in value, depending on their maturity date and duration. How fast could interest rates increase by 1%, you ask? History is riddled with instances where interest rates either increased or decreased by 1% or more in a matter of weeks. As an investor, it's difficult to discern what an abrupt change in market direction means. Does this constitute a short-term anomaly within the current trend or does it constitute a new and different trend that may indicate a true decline in value? For anyone who's currently holding bonds or considering investing more money in bonds, here's something to think about first:

> Bond rates are "at a historic high, 96.1% above the predicted trends. Last time bonds were this high was "in 1940, 86% above the trend. That was the tail end of the Great Depression when investors ran from stocks and piled into bonds. Today bond prices are already above that point."
>
> MarketWatch.com, October 2011

Additionally, Bill Gross, probably the most respected authority on bonds, appears to agree with MarketWatch:

"Unless 100 Years of financial history are meaningless, bonds must go down - and yields and interest rates, up."

What both of these sources are blatantly telling us is bond prices are at historical highs and are ripe for a decline.

When exactly will interest rates start to increase in earnest and drive the price of bonds down? The truthful answer is, I don't know and neither does any financial advisor or market analyst. But unless human history and economic laws cease to exist, it will undoubtedly happen.

The current high level of bonds and their pending decline is the worst-kept secret on earth. When you look at history for clues to the future, the bond market looks like a movie that I've seen before, and I'm pretty sure I know how the movie ends.

Deferring Income Taxes Is Always Best.... Or Is It?

"What is the difference between a taxidermist and a tax collector? The taxidermist takes only your skin."

–Mark Twain

Ever since IRAs and 401(k) plans hit the American landscape in the early 1970s, the financial industry has fed taxpayers and investors a steady diet of "defer your income taxes until you retire." It's only been the last couple of years that investors started to question this "sacred cow."

It's not hard to find a financial article that discusses the virtues of using a traditional IRA versus a Roth IRA or traditional 401(k) versus a Roth 401(k). Let's face the facts: unless you want to risk jail time, you're going to pay taxes on the income you generate. The real question should be, is it better to pay them now and have them behind you, or defer them and pay later.

Back in the 1970s there were no fewer than 25 different federal tax brackets ranging from 14% to 71.75%. During this period in U.S. history, deferring taxes until you retired would have probably resulted in paying less taxes overall. For example, in 1970 if you earned $120,000 you ran a marginal federal tax bracket of 65.60%... Wow!

Now let's assume you retired the next year and your income dropped to $90,000, your tax bracket would also drop to 61.50 %. On today's standards, these tax brackets seem out of this world, but in this example, deferring taxes would have yielded a net tax saving on your tax deferred investments. This made deferring income through your retirement account a better deal.

Now, fast-forward to January 2013. The Bush era tax cuts expired and the tax compromise that came out of Washington left us with seven tax brackets ranging from 10% to 39.6% (see Figure 1, in Chapter 1.) Assuming you had the same taxable income as above, the federal tax bracket would be 28% in both instances. In other words, you're in the same tax bracket while you were working as after you retired. Therefore the tax savings yielded by deferring your taxes until you retired was rendered moot because your tax bracket stayed the same.

Furthermore, even though the taxes levied on your withdrawals were equal to the taxes you saved on the contributions, it probably hurts much more to be taxed after you retire than while you are working. Think about it. In this example, you made $120,000 while working and you were probably much more able to absorb paying taxes with your pre-retirement income than after you've retired, when your income dropped to $90,000. Not only did your income drop $30,000, but you now must pay taxes on all the monies you pull out of your tax-deferred accounts.

When discussing this concept with my clients, I use the following example in order to start the conversation of *"pay-em now or pay-em later."*

Let's say you invested $10,000 in your traditional 401(k) versus a Roth 401(k). Now let's further assume that you're in the 28% tax bracket and your money will earn 7.2% average return.

As you can see in Figure 9, the growth of the investments inside of either type of 401(k) is equal. But if you consider the tax ramifications associated with these retirement plans, the differences can be dramatic. The $10,000 invested in the traditional 401(k) was deductible and produced a tax savings of $2,800 in the year you made the contribution. The money invested in the Roth 401(k) produced no tax deduction in the year you invested your money.

Tax deductions can be a bit like "heroin," once you start using them you get hooked. Keep in mind that using traditional IRAs or 401(k)s, while wonderful saving devices, only defer the taxes! As Figure 9 demonstrates, while the growth within the Traditional and Roth 401(k) both produce spendable dollars, they can be drastically different.

Figure 9

Years	Traditional 401(k)	Roth 401(k)
1	$10,000	$10,000
10	$20,000	$20,000
20	$40,000	$40,000
30	$80,000	$80,000
Taxes	$22,400	$.00
Spendable	$57,600	$80,000
Tax cost	$22,400	$2,800
Net gross return	$57,600	$77,200

They grow to $80,000 over a 30-year period, but the traditional 401(k) is 100% taxable upon distribution. In contrast, the Roth 401(k) is 100% tax-free upon distribution. Keep in mind that similar results will be produced by comparing a traditional IRA and Roth IRA.

So, is it worth $2,800 upfront to save $22,400 down the road?

To truly determine if it's better to pay your taxes today or defer them until retirement, you have to determine two variables, your income at retirement and the future federal tax brackets. It's not difficult to project one's retirement income (we'll discuss this in Chapter 4); it's another thing to predict tax brackets.

The question you should be asking yourself is *"Will taxes be higher after I retire than they are today?"*

No one knows the answer to this question; however, conventional wisdom says tax rates will rise in the future. Over the past couple of years

I've read dozens of articles discussing the current state of the U.S. economy and the fiscal and monetary policies that may be enacted in order to fund our government's spending habits. I cannot remember one of those articles predicting tax rates will stay the same or go down; virtually all of them discuss various methods by which the federal government will increase revenues by changing the tax code.

In 2012, the federal budget was $3.7 trillion and revenues were $2.6 trillion, leaving us with a $1.1 trillion budget deficit. In other words we spent approximately 42% more than we earned. Historically, we borrowed the difference and added it to our national debt, which in March 2013 stands at $16.6 trillion and rising, as indicated in Figure 10.

Figure 10

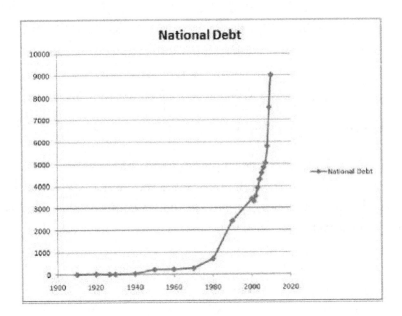

Currently, solutions to our national debt and budget deficit are hotly debated topics in Washington, not to mention the rest of the nation. The optimum level for income tax rates is a point of contention between rival political parties. One believes low tax rates stimulate renewed economic growth, thereby increasing overall tax revenue. The other believes higher income taxes are the best way to raise the revenue the U.S. government requires.

Which philosophy will prevail?

If I were to bet on the outcome, regrettably I have to say I'd bet on higher taxes. Unfortunately economics don't rule Washington..... politics does.

So, whatever your view of the future is, having a frank discussion with your financial advisor regarding the use of financial instruments such as Roth 401(k)s, Roth IRAs, municipal bonds, life insurance and annuities should be on the top of your to-do list.

Buy Stocks. They'll Always Give You the Best Returns

While it's true the stock market has provided the best long-term return of any asset class, it doesn't always work out that way for the average individual investor. As I mentioned earlier, I believe stocks to be a good long-term investment but they shouldn't be relied upon as the sole investment within a retirement account.

The 100-year return of the Dow Jones is roughly 9.4%, about half of which is price growth and the other half is from company dividends. Over the years the investment industry and the financial press have touted these long-term returns as achievable by the individual investor. As we discussed earlier in this chapter, the implication is... all you have to do is buy good stocks or mutual funds, and let the stock market and capitalism do its magic.

How many times have you seen an advertisement for the high returns from a mutual fund or sat down with a financial advisor and come away with a fancy proposal showing a nice double-digit return you're likely to get if you invest your money with their firm?

Well, how many of you have actually experienced those returns or even heard of anybody else experiencing those lofty returns?

Are those mutual fund companies and financial advisors lying to you? Of course not, but what they are doing is showing you "historical returns," which mean almost nothing because you're concerned about future returns. In many cases, mutual fund companies tout last year's best

performing fund as a way to lure you into moving your money to them.
And guess what?

It works.

The advertisements always come with the phrase *"past results are not a guarantee of future results,"* but the implication of future riches always lurk there. History has taught mutual fund companies that these advertising tactics work. When they promote a fund that has performed above average, money comes flying in the door. And in most cases when those returns aren't duplicated, the investor tends to stay with the fund hoping for a repeat performance down the road. Or perhaps they'll switch to another fund within the fund group. Either way, the mutual fund company's goal of attracting and retaining your money worked.

Financial advisors are famous for putting together proposals that include impressive-looking charts and graphs, not to mention the lofty return figures. Are they being disingenuous? Could the investment advisors "cherry pick" the investment funds and investment managers they show you in these proposals? Investment advisors typically have access to literally hundreds if not thousands of different mutual fund companies and private investment managers.

Ask yourself the obvious question. Do you think when the investment advisor prepared a proposal for you, he or she picked the historically best- or worst-performing funds and managers? Of course you're going to see the ones that performed best. It sells.

Unfortunately, research shows the mutual funds that performed best over the most recent time will most probably not repeat that performance in the immediate future. In fact, many of the high flyers are destined to become average or below average performers in the future.

A study done by Lipper in 2003 looked at the top-ranked mutual funds from 1996-1999 and then looked at where those very same mutual funds ranked from 1999-2002. As you might imagine, the top performing funds of the earlier time period produced unenviable returns in the latter time period. The top 10 mutual funds in the years 1996-1999 dropped to an average rank of 818 between the years of 1999-2002. In other words, if you purchased one of the top 10 mutual funds in the earlier time period, chances are there were 808 mutual funds that did better than your fund in the latter time frame.

To exaggerate this point, Srikant Dash, an index strategist at Standard & Poor's, is quoted as saying, *"Very few funds repeat the top quartile performance. Furthermore Standard & Poor's research shows that a healthy percentage, and in most cases a majority of, top quartile funds will in the future most likely come from the ranks of a prior second or third quartiles."*

Here Dash is saying the top-performing funds in the future will most likely not be one of the top-performing funds of the past; in fact the future top performers will most likely come from the ranks of past underachievers.

It's unfortunate many investors fall into the trap of believing the past can be a predictor of the future.

Many investors still hold onto the axiom of "buy-and-hold." As we discussed earlier in this chapter, that strategy is better left for dead. But when one looks at market performance over a period of time, it becomes easy to believe you can "stay the course" and replicate those returns for yourself. As mentioned above, the 100-year rate of return of the Dow Jones is 9.4%. It's true – if you'd bought the 30 Dow stocks, gone to sleep for 100 years and then suddenly awakened, you'd have averaged 9.4%.

To make this happen, you would have had to have held on through the crash of 1929 and the subsequent Great Depression; you would have held tight and not become frustrated as the market traded sideways for 17 years between 1963 and 1982; you wouldn't have panicked on Black Monday in 1987 or during the tech-wreck of 2000-2002; and, most recently, you would have stood your ground during the market decline of 2008-2009 caused by the real estate and mortgage crisis.... Then you'd have made 9.4% average annual return.

Would it have been possible to hold on and not succumb to these economic events? Investor behavior studies tell us the answer is... No.

Volumes have been written on "investor behavior," all attempting to explain why as investors we act and behave the way we do. One of the more popular studies is done annually by Dalbar Inc.. The Boston-based research firm has performed a Quantitative Analysis of Investor Behavior (QAIB) study since 1994. The study is designed to measure the effects of decisions to buy and sell or switch from one mutual fund to another by individual investors over various periods of time. The study looks at the average rate of return of the stock market (S&P 500) over rolling 20-year periods versus the average rate of return of equity mutual fund investors over that same period.

As you might suspect, the market handily outperformed the individual, study after study. The last two published Dalbar studies from 2011 and 2012 show the same pattern of individual investor underperformance. In 2011, the 20-year average for the S&P 500 was 9.14%, while the average rate of return for the individual mutual fund buyer was 3.27%. The 2012 data was similar, with the S&P 500 average 7.81% versus 3.49% for the individual.

So, why the disparity?

The QAIB study displays the consistently poor decisions made by the average individual investor who is determining when to own or not own mutual funds. As the market goes up, attitudes toward accepting risk become more tolerant. After all, if your 401(k) statement made you smile, watching the financial news shows will usually reinforce your decision to hold or perhaps buy more stock funds. But worst of all, individuals tend to become complacent or even a bit arrogant as a positive stock market rewards them. Invariably the complacency leads them to continue buying as the market becomes overvalued.

Subsequently as the market retreats, the average individual investors tend to "hold on" hoping for a market rebound. As the news surrounding the market worsens and it doesn't rebound, the losses become too painful and the individual characteristically sells out and locks in the losses.

You may think it would be easy to avoid these classic pitfalls.... You'd be wrong. Various investor psychology studies have been performed over the years, and most of the conclusions are similar. Individual investors drastically underperformed both the market averages as well as the professional investor.

Remember the comment that Joe Kennedy was rumored to have made in the late 1920s, *"I knew it was time to sell when my shoeshine boy started giving me stock tips."*

Or to quote the famed financier Baron Rothschild, *"It's time to buy when there's blood on the streets, even if it's your own."*

These quotes were true 100 years ago just as they're true today. It's probably a smart bet to lighten up your stock holdings when everything you hear, read and see is positive. And vice versa, when you think things couldn't possibly get worse, you should probably be making a list of which stocks or mutual funds you'd like to own in the near future.

It's very easy to believe you'll be smart enough to *sell* when everyone says *buy* and *buy* when it seems the whole world is *selling*. As the Dalbar studies show.... It isn't.

I Can Manage My Own Money, I Don't Need Any Advice

This may very well be true. After all, it doesn't take a rocket scientist to be a quality investor and achieve solid performance over the long run. However, what I believe most individuals do not appreciate is the time and persistence it takes to be a "good investor."

We've all seen countless television commercials touting that if you....buy our software, log in to our website, buy my book or listen to our advice, we'll be given the methods and secrets of how to outsmart the market.

Well, if you're one of these people, I hate to burst your bubble because none of it is true. If anyone had figured out how to truly "beat the market," do you really think they'd package it and sell it to you for three easy payments of $49.95? Of course not. They just need you to believe they can.

Managing an investment portfolio is hard work and can be monotonous, frustrating and time consuming. After all, it's much more than just looking at closing prices each day. Over the years when meeting with a potential new client, I've asked them how they made their investment decisions regarding what they currently held in their accounts. The answers are many, but they all can be boiled down to a few:

- I researched the mutual fund's history and picked ones that have done best in the past.

- I watched their prices and they seemed to be doing okay.
- I diversified my money because I didn't want too much risk.

All of these appear to be good, logical reasons to buy and hold different investments. In reality, the investment markets are an ever-changing and hostile environment. The market doesn't care who you are, why you are investing your money, when you're going to retire or how much research you've done. The markets are going to change and respond to hundreds of different variables every day.

Over the years I've spoken with dozens of professional money managers, and the one common thread is they're all diligent and detailed, with a strategy for every contingency they may face. For example, if they are considering taking a position in a mutual fund heavy in technology stocks, they'll scrutinize the individual stocks held within the fund and analyze economic events and trends that may affect the technology industry. They'll know the exact price at which they would like to purchase the fund, and, even before they buy, in many cases they'll know the price at which they'd like to sell.

Once the decision to buy is made, they "manage the position," which is to say they analyze the fund and the variables that may affect it daily. In most cases after they've purchased an investment, as a safeguard they'll place a "stop loss" order to protect themselves in case the market and the investment take a sudden dive.

Now, I know that was a very short description of what a real money manager does. But are you willing to do that every day?

I understand analyzing stocks or mutual funds can be empowering and even exciting, but eventually all the excitement wears off and you're left with painstaking hard work. And just because you're being diligent in your efforts doesn't mean you're going to do well. As I've mentioned, history tells us the individual investor doesn't fare well.

After all, do you really think Wall Street's on your side? If you do, you probably also still believe in Santa Claus and the Easter Bunny.

Ideally, working with a competent investment, retirement or financial advisor will help in the creation of a plan that will work specifically for you. They should be used as both a *sounding board and coach* that can keep you moving in the right direction.

After all, even the best like Michael Jordan and Tiger Woods have a coach.

Stay Away from Annuities and Life Insurance

Killing this sacred cow is an ongoing process.

Question: Which is more painful, a root canal or buying life insurance?

Both annuities and life insurance are largely misunderstood and underutilized financial tools. Used properly, they both can have positive influences on most financial and retirement plans. But most of us are apt to crinkle our noses at the suggestion of using one of these tools as part of a financial solution.

This section is not designed to make you run out and buy the first life insurance policy or annuity you come across. What I'm trying to get across is that there are many financial tools at our disposal and they all have different features, benefits, strengths and weaknesses. It's up to us as investors to educate ourselves and understand what these various tools can do to help us achieve our financial goals.

Stocks, bonds, mutual funds, CDs, real estate, commodities, money market accounts, precious metals, life insurance and annuities are all distinctly different financial tools and can play a role in helping achieve our financial objectives. They come with different risk levels, liquidity features and tax considerations; it's up to you and your Financial Advisor to use them wisely.

The poor reputation of annuities and life insurance is not completely undeserved. For years both were plagued by high pressure sales, unscrupulous tactics and unsavory salesman. Over the past 10 to 20 years, the industry has made a concerted effort to make amends for their past sins, but many of their past transgressions still exist in the minds of the general public.

Life insurance and annuities have enviable tax advantages and, in most cases, principal guarantees that many other financial products can't offer. It would be shortsighted to write-off their potential because of past indiscretions.

Remember the "risk shifting" discussion in Chapter 1? Used properly, life insurance and annuities are very effective ways to transfer risk from your retirement accounts back to the investment companies.

One of the main themes in *Retiring in America: It's All About the Income* is how an individual investor can put together a retirement plan that offers a level of sustainable income to support their lifestyle for the rest of their lives. The proper use of annuities and life insurance can greatly enhance this effort.

Three types of assets can provide guaranteed lifetime income: Pensions, Social Security and annuities.

Annuities

Annuities are designed to allow tax-deferred growth and future stable income streams. Their bad rap has come as a result of years of low returns, high fees and lack of liquidity. Fortunately, the problems that plagued annuities in the past have led to more innovative product designs that allow for better returns, enhanced liquidity options and lower fee structures than many other investment choices. We'll discuss the various uses annuities can provide in building a solid retirement income plan in Chapter 3, but for now I'll restrict my comments to their structure.

When most people think of annuities they tend to lump them together, when in fact there are several types with countless variations. I tell clients that annuities are like cars. They all have similarities such as tires, engines and steering wheels, but after that, options that make one car preferable over another are numerous.

Annuities come in three basic flavors: Immediate, variable and fixed.

Immediate annuity is the one that comes to mind when most investors visualize "an annuity." Immediate annuity is a trade; you trade a sum of money for a guaranteed income stream. That income stream can be for a specific period of time, say 10 or 20 years, or perhaps for life. Although there are many variations of an immediate annuity, by and large, they're used to supply a sustainable income stream.

Although they're about as exciting as watching grass grow, the immediate annuity can have an important role within a retirement plan. Its stability and relatively high level of income make it an attractive choice for the individual who desires steady reliable income. However, the negatives are that once you've made the decision to use an immediate annuity, you're stuck and can't change your mind later. The immediate annuity is a contract between you and the insurance company.

A *Variable Annuity or VA* is a type of deferred annuity where you invest money in an annuity and defer income until a later date. The growth that occurs while you're deferring income is also deferred from income tax, making it a somewhat efficient vehicle to accumulate retirement savings. The investment choices in VA's are typically a large variety of mutual funds also called subaccounts. As an investor you can structure a diversified portfolio using the various funds made available within the VA and benefit or suffer based on the future stock market direction.

The VA's main claim to fame is that it allows otherwise taxable investment options (mutual funds) to be held inside a tax-efficient vehicle. Held *outside* of a variable annuity, the dividends and capital gains generated by mutual funds are taxable in the year they're recognized. But *inside* the variable annuity those very same dividends and capital gains are tax-deferred, allowing for more efficient growth. But keep in mind the taxes are just deferred; as distributions are made, IRS code mandates the gains come out first and be taxed at ordinary income rates.

The bad news about variable annuities is their high fees. In many cases the annual fees within a variable annuity range from 2 to 4%, making it more difficult to achieve a competitive return. Additionally, capital gains and dividends are typically given preferential tax treatment. In most cases, the maximum federal tax on long-term capital gains is 15%. But as I mentioned above, the tax deferral of capital gains and dividends within a variable annuity causes them to be taxed as *ordinary income*. Typically, the ordinary income rates will be clearly higher than the rates given to capital gains and dividends, thereby minimizing the benefit of the tax-deferred growth offered by the VA.

The *Fixed Annuity or FA* in many cases is the most simple of all. The structure is similar to that of a certificate of deposit. You place your money on deposit for a specific period of time with an insurance company, and in turn you're guaranteed a fixed annual return. And like a CD, the FA has an early termination fee, which typically is the only cost within an FA. It should be noted that fixed annuities are considered safe investments although they do not offer FDIC insurance as with the traditional CD.

A fixed annuity will typically offer a slightly higher fixed return than a comparable CD of the same length. The primary advantages of the FA are its safety, fixed interest rate and tax deferral. For the conservative investor, they can offer a viable choice over comparable fixed income investments such as short-term bonds and CDs.

The negatives of the FA are the same negatives that come with purchasing comparable alternatives, low interest rates and penalties for early withdrawals.

The fixed annuity also has a hybrid cousin the *Fixed Indexed Annuity or FIA*. This annuity is a cross between the fixed annuity and the variable annuity. Its principal is guaranteed, similar to the FA, but the interest is calculated based on the growth of a stock market index (in most cases the S&P 500).

The FIA offers investors safety and the possibility of long-term growth based on the growth of the stock market. The growth usually is limited to an annual maximum called the "Cap Rate." For example, let's say the current cap rate is 7% and the S&P 500 increases 5% during your account year. In this case your account is credited with a 5% return. On the other hand if the S&P 500 grew 10%, you receive the cap of 7%.

One of the most important qualities of the FIA is its no-loss guarantee. We all know the stock markets have good and bad years. As we just showed above, in the positive years your account receives all or part of those gains. In the years the stock market falls, the FIA *does not* lose value. Your principal will not decline because of market corrections nor will any of the past gains credited to your account ever be lost.

When I explain FIA's to a client, I ask: *"You give up some of the gains in the good years in order to have no losses in the bad years. Are you okay with that?"*

The FIA is also a low-cost investment choice. Because your gains come in the form of interest, not capital gains as in variable annuities and mutual funds, there are typically neither management fees nor trading costs.

Many variable, fixed and fixed indexed annuities come with a "guaranteed income rider." These allow the annuity to provide future guaranteed income based on a fixed annual return, which increases its "income base" each year until you decide you want to start your income. These income riders are very useful when planning retirement income because you'll know exactly how much income you'll have at any future date. We'll discuss them further in Chapter 3.

Life Insurance

What if I told you that you could place your money in an account where its principal would be safe, its growth tax-deferred, it remains completely liquid and when you decide you would like to take withdrawals, they'd be income tax free if done correctly. Would this get your attention?

Well, I just described an investment-grade *life insurance policy.*

Over the past several years life insurance companies purposefully redesigned many of their policies to not only provide life insurance protection but allow the policy to act as an investment- and income-producing vehicle.

If you give a good carpenter a hammer, they'll build you a house. If you give a competent financial advisor a good life insurance policy, they'll build an account that can benefit you in areas such as asset protection, retirement income, estate planning and college planning to name a few. Unfortunately, most financial advisors fail to understand or appreciate the nuances available within life insurance.

Life insurance is not an investment in the sense that most people envision. Generally, a life insurance policy is not a vehicle where you would invest a single chunk of money and then sit back and watch it grow similar to a stock, CD or real estate. It should be thought of as a "program" that if set up properly and consistently fed and monitored will produce the desired outcome.

The big drawback for a life insurance policy is.... the insurance. The face amount or death benefit of the policy comes with a cost. This cost of insurance, or COI, as with costs and fees inside of any investment, is a drag on its rate of return. Depending on your health, age and gender, the COI can range from reasonable to ridiculous. In order for a life insurance policy to be an effective retirement planning tool, it helps if you're in reasonably good health.

The idea behind using a life policy as a financial tool is to "over fund" the policy. This is done by putting additional monies in the policy over and above the COI. Let's say the COI for a $200,000 face amount policy is $100 per month. Instead of depositing $100 per month, you may put in $500 per month. The additional $400 goes directly into the "cash value" of the policy. This cash value can be invested in ways similar to the annuity. It can be put in mutual fund subaccounts, fixed interest accounts or index accounts similar to the FIAs discussed above.

Life insurance enjoys powerful tax advantages. IRS code section 801 allows tax-free "inside buildup" within life insurance policies. IRS code section 72(e)(5)(A) allows tax-free borrowing from policies. Actually, you're borrowing against your death benefit, which is tax-free because of IRC 101(a)(1).

We'll tackle more about annuities and life insurance in Chapter 3.

It can be difficult to fight conventional wisdom and not fall prey to herd mentality. However, doing so will let you focus in on what's truly important... you.

Killing the sacred cows of investing will allow you to design a retirement plan that may not work for anyone else on the planet. But if it works for you, that's all that matters.

It's All About Income...

This is by far the most important chapter of this book. As I discussed in the forward, having sufficient income to support one's lifestyle throughout retirement is the goal of most retirement savers. The goal of this book is to help you accomplish that and to get you to think a bit *outside the box*. Now it's time to discuss various methods and techniques to build and sustain consistent income that can last throughout your retirement years.

Income shouldn't be looked at as an absolute number. It should be viewed as the amount of *cash flow* you need in order to pay your bills and accommodate your lifestyle, after taxes, debt and inflation. If you underestimate the effects of future taxes and inflation, you'll find yourself with less *cash flow* to support your lifestyle. In other words, you'll have less money for life's pleasures such as vacations, new cars, dining out and spoiling grandchildren.

There are two sides of the ledger when it comes to cash flow, the income side and the expense side. The income side is obviously the amount of money you're receiving from all income sources. The expense side is your bills, expenses and debt payments. What's left over is what business owners call "free cash flow" and that's what pays for your lifestyle.

You see, cash flow or free cash flow should be thought of as how much money you have left to spend as you wish. By reducing your tax liability and your debt load, you'll obviously have more money left to spend on lifestyle. Therefore, concentrating on reducing debt and taxes is a great way to increase your income.

Andy Barkate

Less Debt Equals More Income

Today, there are three kinds of people: the have's, the have-not's and the have-not-paid-for-what-they have's."

–Earl Wilson

Remember back in the '80s and '90s when it was vogue to borrow money and hold large amounts of debt? Well, thanks to the mortgage and banking crisis of 2008-09, all that's changed. When you're approaching your retirement years, carrying debt is a liability. Everyone serious about planning for a long, fruitful retirement should also have a debt reduction plan as well as a retirement plan in place. I believe that debt reduction or elimination is one of the most essential goals anyone serious about saving toward retirement should be focused on.

Effectively controlling your debt will not only allow you to save and invest more frequently, but it will allow you to have more money available to pay for your lifestyle.

I can't tell you how many times over the years I've designed a retirement plan for a couple and, during the data collection process, discovered their debt payments are the majority of their expenses. For example, monthly expenses might be $6000; of that, the mortgage payment and car payments are over $3000. After they've paid their monthly debts, they still have to buy things like food, clothes, utilities and gasoline. This leaves precious few dollars to save for retirement and to fund your lifestyle.

So, how can you pay down debt? Better yet, how can you pay down debt *fast?*

The best way I've come across to accomplish this is to systematically attack paying off one debt at a time. This approach is known as double-down, snowball or power-down, and hopefully this is not the first time you've heard these concepts. It's an extremely simple and effective approach. You simply continue paying your debts on their normal schedules. The important factor is when you pay off one of your debts, you take the money you were using to pay that debt and apply it to another debt, effectively doubling-down. In order to have this method work effectively you must avoid the temptation of spending the money created

51

by paying off the first debt. Figures 11 and 12 will help you understand the power of using this debt reduction concept.

Figure 11

Description	Monthly payment	Interest Rate	Number of payments	Remaining debt	Real debt
Visa	$125	12%	143	$9,500	$17,927
MasterCard	$155	10%	212	$15,400	$32,872
Medical bills	$262	6%	18	$4,500	$4,717
Car payment	$833	6.5%	30	$23,000	$24,981
Home mortgage	$,1276	4.5%	340	$245,000	$433,915
Total Payments	$2,651			$297,400	$514,413
Total interest payments					$217,013
Years to be Debt Free			28.35		

Figure 12

Description	Principal	Monthly Payment	Double-down payments	Interest Rate	Number of payments	Payoff date
Visa	$9,500	$125	0.00	12%	144	April 2025
MasterCard	$15,400	$155	$125	10%	177	January 2028
Medical bills	$4,500	$262	$280	6%	19	November 2014
Car payment	$23,000	$832	$542	6.5%	28	August 2015
Home mortgage	$245,000	$1,276	$1,375	4.5%	152	December 2015
Total Payments		$2,651				$407,702
Total interest payments						$110,302
Years to be Debt Free					14.76	

As you can see, Figure 11 depicts an individual with various amounts of debt and paying it down on schedule. It will take approximately 28.35 years to pay off all debts, and during that period of time he or she will have paid over $217,000 worth of interest.

By contrast, Figure 12 displays the concept of doubling-down. The "Doubling-Down payment" column illustrates retiring one specific debt, then adding that debt's monthly payment to the monthly payment of another debt in order to pay it off more rapidly. By using this method, your debts are completely retired in 14.76 years, almost half the time shown in figure 10. Additionally, your total interest payments fall to $110,302 resulting in $106,711 of savings.

What could you do with additional $106,711?

You could spend it, but hopefully you'll save and invest it.

Keep in mind that when using this strategy you should consider the order in which you pay off debts. In most cases, the debts with the highest interest rates should be paid down first. However, in many cases, debts with high monthly payments or the fewest remaining payments can be attacked first in order to free up larger amounts of cash to pay down subsequent debts. Also, attention should be given to debts that have interest payments which are tax-deductible, such as those attached to home mortgages. These debts typically carry lower interest rates along with being deductible and should be paid down after other non-deductible debts are paid off.

An important concept to understand about the Double-Down system is that you are drastically accelerating the payment of your debts using the *same amount of money*. In both Figures 11 and 12, the total monthly payments are $2651 (the same amount of money!). The only difference is how you're using this monthly expenditure. In many cases, as an individual pays off a debt, he or she simply consumes the additional cash flow. In the Double-Down system that additional cash flow is used to pay off debt, which requires more discipline.

Discipline has its rewards. Not only are you out of debt almost 14 years sooner, but think about what you can do with the monthly cash flow you would have normally used the to pay those debts.

What if you invested it?

At the end of 14.76 years, let's take the $2,651 debt payment and invest it over the time period it would have taken you to pay off your debt in Figure 11 (28.35 years). You could generate the tidy sum of $573,215, assuming you earned a 4% annual return. Not bad.

Is it Your Retirement Account or Uncle Sam's?

"I am proud to be paying taxes in the United States. The only thing is – I could be just as proud for half the money."
— Arthur Godfrey

Supreme Court Justice Oliver Wendell Holmes once said "Taxes are what we pay for a civilized society." While I believe Justice Holmes makes a good point, if he were alive today he might view things a bit more like Mr. Godfrey.

There are over 50 different types of tax our government levies upon us. When you add them all together, it is most likely over 50% of your income that goes to taxes in one form or another. Therefore, making an effort to *legally* lower the amount of taxes you pay will leave you with more money to fund your lifestyle.

While some of these taxes are lesser-known, such as taxes on utilities, telephones and building permits, we will focus on methods to reduce taxes that affect your income and assets, such as income tax, estate tax and taxes on capital gains, interest and dividends.

In Chapter 2, we discussed Traditional and Roth IRAs and 401(k)s, as well as life insurance and annuities. Each of these financial tools has tax benefits and by extension have income benefits associated with them. I gave examples of the long-term tax benefits of using a Roth 401(k) or Roth IRA.

Now, let's use the same example discussed in Chapter 2 (Figure 9) to discuss income. Figure 9 displays the difference between paying your taxes now versus deferring them and paying them later. We show investing $10,000 today and allowing it to grow to $80,000 over 30 years (7.2% interest). In this example, both IRA types have the same account balances, but the after-tax income generated is drastically different.

54

Assuming a 5% withdrawal rate, both IRAs and 401(k)s will produce $4,000 annually. However, the income from the Traditional IRA and 401(k) is taxable. The income from the Roth IRA and 401(k) is tax-free.

Assuming you still pay in the 28% tax bracket after you retire (highly unlikely), your after-tax spendable money produced by the IRA or 401k is $2,880.

Because all income generated in the Roth IRA or Roth 401(k) is tax-free, the net spendable income is $4,000.

In this example you invested $10,000 and paid tax of $2,800 in year one. When you start taking income, you're saving $1,120 in taxes *every year!* Your upfront cost (taxes) is paid back in spades.

Now let's make it even more interesting. Let's assume you are investing $10,000 *per year* in your 401(k), IRA or TSP (TSP is the Federal Government's 401k). How does the Traditional plan compare to the Roth plan?

Figure 13

Years	Traditional 401(k)	Roth 401(k)
1	$10,000	$10,000
10	$149,519	$149,519
20	$449,189	$449,189
30	$1,049,798	$1,049,798
Taxes on contribution	$.00	$84,000
5% income	$52,490	$52,490
After-tax income, 28% federal taxes	$37,793	$52,490
Net income over 20 years	$755,855	$1,049,800

Although the traditional 401(k), IRA or TSP allowed you to deduct the $10,000 per year contribution from your current income, the after-tax cash flow from the Roth version is much higher.

If you're willing to give up the $2,800 per year tax deduction associated with the Traditional 401(k) ($84,000 total tax savings over 30 years), your annual increase in spendable income is $14,697 ($52,490 less $37,793). Look at it another way. It took you 30 years to save $84,000 in federal income taxes by investing $10,000 per year in a Traditional retirement account. When you started taking income from this traditional plan, it took you less than 5 ½ years to pay back all the taxes you'd saved by deducting your contributions for 30 years.

So....... Whose retirement plan is it anyway...... Yours or Washington's?

In order to drive home this point a bit further, consider the net income over 20 Years in Figure 13. The difference between the total incomes of the Traditional versus Roth plans is $293,945... Wow. Remember, it cost you $84,000 in federal taxes to use the Roth plan versus the traditional. Which one seems like the best deal to you?

Keep in mind that I'm assuming a constant 28% federal income tax bracket. If you're lucky enough to live in a state that levies a state income tax, the Roth retirement plans will produce even more after-tax income than their Traditional counterparts.

As you can see, Roth 401(k)s, TSP and IRA accounts can produce a superior after-tax retirement income, which fits well in our goal of creating enough predictable and sustainable income to support our lifestyles throughout retirement.

Roth retirement accounts can provide enhanced income planning opportunities. Because the income coming from Roth accounts is tax-free, this can allow you to structure your income payments in a more tax-efficient manner.

For example, if you had both a Roth and Traditional IRA and needed additional cash from one of these accounts to supply additional retirement income, the tax-free income from the Roth IRA will allow you to control and reduce your annual taxable income.

As a financial and retirement planner, I routinely discuss tactics to not only build and increase retirement income, but arrange income in a way that will be the most tax efficient.

Here's a basic example. John and Mary Smith need $6,000 after-tax per month to fund their retirement lifestyle. Between their pensions and Social Security benefits, they'll have $4,000 after tax per month, meaning they'll need an additional $2,000 after-tax. John and Mary have both Traditional and Roth IRAs.

From which accounts should they take the remaining $2,000 per month they'll need?

Because you're reading this book, it shows you're not only interested in your retirement but you're obviously inquisitive, so you've already figured out that taking the money from the Roth is the best alternative.

The $2,000 taken from the Roth IRA is tax-free, meaning that John and Mary will receive the additional income they need without incurring additional taxes. On the other hand, if they withdrew $2,000 per month from the Traditional IRA, they'd be taxed on this additional income. In order to clear $2,000 monthly, they'd have to take out approximately $3,000 a month from their Traditional IRA.

In order to state the obvious, John and Mary will receive $72,000 of after-tax income by using the Roth versus the Traditional retirement account as a current income source. This not only reduces their annual income tax expense, it allows the Traditional IRA to grow to be used at a later date, if necessary.

It should also be noted that Traditional IRAs and 401(k) plans involve a Required Minimum Distribution (RMD) when you reach the age of 70 ½. This forces you to take money from these plans and pay taxes, whether you want to or not. Strategies can be employed to best use these forced distributions.

On the other hand, the Roth IRA has no RMD mandate. Therefore your money can continue to grow tax-free until you decide you'd like to use it.

The Roth 401(k) is a bit different. Money within a Roth 401(k) is subject to the RMD rules, but the distributions are still tax-free.

Roth IRAs and 401(k)s have estate benefits that their Traditional counterparts don't. As we've already discussed, because the investment in Roth IRA and 401(k) is after tax, all the growth and income is tax free. This allows beneficiaries of Roth plans to have choices the beneficiaries of Traditional plans don't.

For example, the Pension Protection Act of 2006 (PPA) made it possible for the beneficiary of a Roth 401(k) to roll over plan assets into an inherited Roth IRA. Additionally, the beneficiary of a Roth IRA can also roll over the plan into an inherited Roth IRA.

This is important to understand because the beneficiary of a Traditional IRA cannot roll over the inherited IRA into an inherited Roth IRA... go figure.

Keep in mind the beneficiary of a Roth 401(k) or IRA must either continue or start RMDs, but those distributions are tax free. Additionally, during the RMD period the remaining balance within the inherited Roth IRA is compounding tax free.

This allows beneficiaries to maintain flexibility over the inherited Roth IRA. They may invest their money in a manner that fits their risk tolerance, including, stocks, bonds, mutual funds, CDs, annuities, precious metals, real estate, etc. Additionally, the beneficiaries can withdraw monies at their discretion (other than the RMDs) without paying taxes.

By contrast, the PPA allows beneficiaries of a Traditional 401(k) to convert the plan assets directly into an inherited Roth IRA. But this conversion is taxable!

If we use the example in Figure 13, the $1,049,798 balance in the Traditional 401(k) would be taxed as it was converted into an inherited Roth IRA..... Ouch!

Oddly enough, depending on the circumstances this might be the most appropriate strategy for a beneficiary to take.

It should be noted that in order for a beneficiary to roll over a 401(k) into a Traditional inherited IRA or an inherited Roth IRA, it must be a *direct transfer*. If the beneficiary makes the mistake of receiving the distribution directly, they'll lose the opportunity to roll over the assets into an inherited IRA or inherited Roth IRA and to *stretch out* the account. On the top of that, the IRS will expect you to write a very large check for federal income taxes due.

Over the years I've dealt with the beneficiaries of many of our clients' retirement accounts. In most circumstances the use of the accounts is greatly restricted because of tax consequences. In other words, if the beneficiary would like to pull out a chunk of money from the inherited account, the tax liability can make the distribution unwise.

In the Roth retirement account, the beneficiary will not pay taxes on any of the distributions they receive. That allows them to use their inheritance in any manner they choose without fear of paying taxes.

If you think about it, most of you would probably want your beneficiaries to have access to their inheritance in order to improve their lives.

And you thought 401(k)'s and IRAs were simple...

As you can see, using retirement accounts correctly will not only save you large amounts of money that would ordinarily go to the IRS, but it will also give your beneficiaries more flexibility.

Make sure you consult a well-trained financial advisor with experience in retirement plans. Pick their brains and formulate a strategy that works best for you and your family.

Roth Conversions

Roth IRA and 401(k) accounts are relatively new beasts. Most of you have primarily used the Traditional plans. Over the past few years, much has been written about Roth conversions. Should you convert your traditional 401(k), TSP or IRA into a Roth?

The answer is..... it depends.

First of all, converting a Traditional retirement account into a Roth retirement account entails paying income taxes, which is enough to cause most of us to lose interest. Until 2010, the possibility of converting the Traditional plan into a Roth plan was dependent upon your adjusted gross income (AGI). In 2009, if your AGI was above $100,000, you could not convert your traditional IRA into a Roth. However, the PPA permanently did away with the income limitation in 2010.

Roth 401(k)'s and IRAs have definite estate planning advantages, as we discussed. But does it make financial sense to convert an existing traditional 401(k), TSP or IRA into a Roth? The answer is not simple. I believe the correct decision depends upon the motives of the individual.

For example, if you have adequate assets and income sources so you won't need your Traditional plan as an income source in retirement, then you may justify the Roth conversion on the grounds that paying your taxes *now* will allow the Roth account to grow tax-free and avoid RMDs in the future. Additionally, the estate advantages are greatly enhanced by using the Roth.

On the other hand, if your current game plan is to use your retirement accounts to augment your income during retirement, then the decision is a bit more difficult. Is it worth converting your traditional retirement plan into a Roth and paying the taxes, thereby turning the account balance of a traditional account into a smaller account balance of a Roth retirement account?

The answer is...... it depends.

In my view it depends primarily on one variable: future income tax rates.

It's really a math problem. If the income tax rate you pay on the conversion today is lower than future income tax rates, the conversion will yield higher after-tax annual income.

Remember, our goal in this book is to show you ways to create sustainable retirement income.

Let's look at an example using the same numbers as in Figure 13 to discuss this point. Say you've been contributing $10,000 to a traditional 401(k) for 20 years, earning 7.2% annually, ending with an account balance of $449,189. Then you convert into a Roth 401(k) at the 28% federal tax bracket.

First of all, there is no rule on how many years you take to convert to a Roth. You may convert all in one year or stretch it out over several. You must be conscious of how much you're converting annually because this amount will be added to your taxable income, possibly pushing you into a higher federal and state tax brackets. Running multiple scenarios can give you a clearer picture of both your current tax liability and your future income.

As Figure 14 displays, if your income tax bracket remains unchanged over time, the after-tax income on both the Traditional and Roth 401(k) are equal. Over the 10 and 20 year time period, the after-tax incomes are $32,410 and $64,957 respectively. Therefore, the Roth conversion does not yield an advantage.

However, if tax brackets increased 28% to 35% by the time you retired, the after-tax income of the Roth 401(k) is superior. The Traditional 401(k) would yield income of $29,259 and $58,642 over the 10 and 20 year time respectively, versus the $32,410 and $64,957 for the Roth 401(k). As you've probably surmised, determining if converting your retirement account to a Roth is a wise financial move is dependent upon assumptions that you and your advisor make. It's important those assumptions are both conservative and realistic. And even then, there's no guarantee of what the future will hold.

Now let's consider the long-term implications of a Roth conversion. While it's difficult to bite the tax bullet and convert it into a Roth all at once, let's look at an example of a *partial conversion* and the long-term income implications for you and your family.

Figure 14

	Traditional 401(k)	Roth 401(k) conversion	Income Traditional 401(k) 28% tax bracket	Income Traditional 401(k) 35%tax bracket	Income Roth IRA
Current value	$449,187	$323,406			
10 year value	$900,280	$648,201	$32,410	$29,259	$32,410
20 year value	$1,804,370	$1,299,146	$64,957	$58,642	$64,957

Note: Income assumes a 5% withdrawal rate

If you and your spouse are both 65 years old and have a $500,000 traditional IRA or 401(k), converting it to a Roth all in the same year would most likely result in state and federal taxation of close to 45 to 50%.

Let's assume your spouse is the primary beneficiary of both accounts (Traditional and Roth) and your 40-year-old son is the contingent beneficiary. Now suppose you live a long fruitful life and pass away at 85 and your spouse inherits both accounts and subsequently passes away at age 90. Your son, who is now 65, inherits the traditional IRA and must continue RMDs. Over this extended period of years, the original $500,000 IRA would have produced $1,617,762 of income assuming it earned 5% annual return. So, for every $1.00 dollar in the IRA, it produced $3.24 of income. Not bad.

Keep in mind the $3.24 is before tax.

Okay, let's think long-term and outside the box. What if you converted 10% or $50,000 of your $500,000 Traditional IRA into a Roth IRA? Keep in mind the money left in your traditional IRA is subject to RMDs, thereby slowly depleting its value. Also, remember the Roth IRA has no RMD requirement. Because of this the Roth IRA grows to $169,321 prior to your son inheriting it.

The RMDs taken from the Roth IRA over your son's lifetime amount to $295,695. For every $1.00 placed in the Roth IRA, almost $5.91 was returned to your family. Tax free!

Keep in mind, on top of this Roth income, you've still got the reminding income coming from the Traditional IRA you didn't convert to the Roth.

Now let's give the example a twist. Let's assume that your 9-year-old grandson is the beneficiary in lieu of your 40-year-old son. Because your grandson's life expectancy is much longer than your son's, the RMD tables are further stretched out.

The original $50,000 converted to the Roth account will have produced approximately $700,000 of tax-free income for your grandson over his life expectancy. Now, that might not only pay for a college education but leave a meaningful legacy.

If you compare the long-term income benefit to your family, the Roth IRA, 401(k) or TSP wins hands-down.

Portfolio Income

Traditionally, most retirement accounts are invested in assets that have market exposure, such as stocks, bonds and mutual funds. Much research has been done on using these types of assets to produce retirement income.

The market can be an effective way to invest money, but for retirement planning purposes it must be held in proper perspective.

The stock market has provided the most generous long-term growth of any asset class. However, because of its volatility and unpredictable nature its use within an income portfolio has proven to be problematic. In order to be less vulnerable an investor should strike the proper balance between the amount of risky assets they hold (stocks, bonds and mutual funds) and safe assets which have no market risk. The proper balance depends on the amount of income you need from your portfolio as well as your risk tolerance.

Keep in mind this book is about producing sustainable sources of income, not analyzing and selecting which stocks to buy. As a result, I judge portfolios on the merit of producing income in a consistent manner. Because of the volatile nature of these types of assets, income planning becomes a bit trickier.

In Chapter 2, we discussed the "4% rule." For anyone attempting to use market driven assets to produce long-term retirement income, the 4% rule must be understood. This rule is defined as the percentage withdrawal rate that a portfolio consisting of stocks and bonds can reasonably withstand without depleting. Research on this theory indicates the optimal percentage allocation between stocks and bonds is 60/40. This allocation produces the highest level of income that can be withdrawn from a portfolio while standing a reasonable chance of lasting throughout a 30-year retirement period, without running dry.

However, the research also indicates that depending upon economic and market fluctuations, the 4% withdrawal rate could be either increased or decreased. If you look at the Bill and Bob example in Chapter 2, it becomes apparent that "timing" can play a large part in the annual distribution rate your portfolio can't handle.

An article by Wade Pfau, Ph.D., in the August 2011 issue of the *Journal of Financial Planning*, titled *"Can We Predict the Sustainable Withdrawal Rate for New Retirees,"* discussed the range of withdrawal rates over various periods of time and found them to be significantly different.

In this paper, Pfau used the same 60% stock, 40% bond allocation as William Bergen used in formulating his 4% Rule.

Phau's research indicated that in order to have a solid chance of *not* running out of money over a 30-year retirement, the year in which you retired played a major role. For example, if you started retirement in 1966, you could have withdrawn 3.53% annually. On the other hand, if you retired in 1921 or 1922, the withdrawal rate could have been as high as 10%. Too bad Mr. Pfau's research wasn't around for my great-grandfather.

The paper goes on to predict safe withdrawal rates for recent retirees. The author stated that if you retired in the year 2000, the withdrawal rate should be 2.7%, it drops to 1.5% and 1.8% if you retired in 2008 or 2010 respectively.

The 4% Rule is a theory, not an economic law. It was formulated in the 1980s when interest rates were substantially higher than they are now. More recent research, such as Pfau's, suggests that the current low interest rate environment and recent stock market volatility means the 4% theory should be adjusted down.

A report published by *Morningstar* in January 2013 also criticized the 4% rule. This report cited low bond yields as a primary reason for sustainable withdrawal rates set closer to 2.8%. It goes on to say that a 4% withdrawal rate has a 50% chance of success over a 30-year retirement. Said another way, if you and your best friend plan on taking 4% from your retirement accounts annually, chances are one of you will wind up penniless.

The *Morningstar* report does offer a recommendation to those who desire a 4% withdrawal rate.... save more money!

The report recommended in order to sustain a 4% withdrawal rate, your retirement account balance should be 42.9% higher than an account balance required to allow an 2.8% withdrawal rate.

For decades economists and financial academics have worked to understand the optimum allocation between stocks and bonds that provides the best possible result for individuals using their life savings for income. And the 4% rule is the best they can do....Really?

So... you must be willing to shoulder the risk of market collapses, bond defaults, interest rate swings and unforeseen economic events, in order to get a 4% income. You must be kidding?

I'm not sure about you, but I think that stinks. There's got to be a better way.

If you read a few of the articles written discussing the 4% rule, you may come to the same conclusion I did: If the most I can expect from a retirement account invested in stocks and bonds is around 4%, perhaps investing the majority of my money in the market isn't the smartest thing to do.

Understanding historical data and future predictions is important if you have the nerve to use market-driven assets as part of your retirement income solution. The 4% rule and the research surrounding it will give you a much more accurate guide than relying on the fancy proposals and illustrations provided by most financial advisors and investment companies.

A viable alternative to the 4% rule and the somewhat random diversification strategies of many retirement minded investors as well as their financial advisors is "Modern Portfolio Theory" or MPT.

MPT is the science of risk-adjusted asset allocation. Pioneered by Harry Markowitz's back in the 1980s, it helped him win the Nobel Prize for economics in 1990.

MPT explains that every level of risk has an optimal asset allocation that will maximize returns over the long run. It also suggests that asset allocation is superior to selecting individual investments or attempting to time the market. Additionally MPT discusses the concept of "correlation" within an investment portfolio.

Correlation can be most easily described as how closely the values of different asset classes or investments move in relationship to each other. Here's an example; in your IRA account you might have two mutual funds. Both funds invest in stocks trading on the US stock market. Even though these funds are from different investment companies and have different investment objectives, they're both playing in the same pond (US stocks). Therefore, these two investments will be highly correlated to each other. In other words, they will increase or decrease in value at very similar rates.

MPT argues that a well-diversified portfolio will consist of assets that possess a high degree of *non-correlation*. Keep in mind that its goal is to gain the optimum return at a given risk level. Said another way; what is the return an investor can expect given the level of risk they're willing to take. MPT argues that proper asset allocation can enhance the relationship between risk and return.

The role that correlation or non-correlation plays within a diversified portfolio is a concept I believe most investors fail to appreciate. Many times I see the investment choices that individuals make within their retirement plans (401(k), TSP or IRA) in an attempt to be diversified. In most cases they believe they're adequately diversified because their accounts are split between a couple of stock and bond mutual funds.

Unfortunately, these investments are principally investing in simpler asset class thereby making them highly correlated to one another. Just think back a few years ago when the markets were falling because of the mortgage crisis. It didn't really matter which type of stock or stock fund you owned, they all fell in value because they're all highly correlated to each other.

In an attempt to control volatility, many investors add bonds into the mix. This is the remedy prescribed by most financial advisors in order to add stability within a portfolio. This approach sounds great but regrettably it doesn't work all that well. If you had an allocation of stocks and bonds in your retirement account in 2008, did this buffer the fall your portfolio sustained? In volatile market cycles, stocks and bonds have proven to be more highly correlated than originally thought.

In order to create a portfolio that is probably diversified, one must use assets that are non-correlated to one another. This is not easy to do in most retirement plans because the investment choices (mutual funds) tend to be correlated. Most veteran investment advisers will tell you to add areas which have a low correlation to stocks and bonds such as precious metals, commodities, real estate, annuities and cash in order to build a portfolio that is correctly diversified.

If you use an investment advisor to help you with your choices, you may ask them if your portfolio was constructed using MPT standards. If they give you a blank stare when you mention concepts like MPT or correlation, this probably means you may have a hodgepodge of investments which were recommended without any serious thought. This could explain why your account values soared when times were good only to crash right along with the markets.

The horrific market decline of 2007- 2008 has led to a tremendous market rally which currently has both the S&P 500 and Dow Jones near all-time highs. Using MPT to guide you in your diversification strategy will undoubtedly save a lot of pain during economic declines while allowing your retirement accounts to flourish in good times.

As you can probably guess, I'm not a large proponent of relying on risky assets to provide consistent income in retirement. It's not that stocks and bonds can't play a part of the retirement plan, but in my view they should play a diminished role because their future values and cash flows can't be adequately predicted.

Annuities... Yeah, I Actually Said Annuities

As I stated in Chapter 2, only three asset categories provide guaranteed income for life: Social Security, pensions and... annuities.

We discussed annuities a bit in Chapter 2. Now let's dig a bit beneath the surface of these accounts to see what they can contribute to retirement income.

At its core, the annuity is designed to be an asset that provides income that you cannot outlive. This feature makes the annuity an important tool when it comes to building a retirement portfolio designed to supply consistent income throughout your retired years.

Let's look at a few instances where annuities can be used within a retirement account to achieve a goal of long-term stable income.

We'll start with something simple. Let's say you and your spouse retire at age 62 and need $5,000 per month to maintain your lifestyle in retirement. Your company pension and Social Security benefits total $3,000 per month, leaving you with an income gap of $2,000.

Additionally, between you and your spouse's 401(k)s, you've managed to save $600,000. To provide a guaranteed income of $2,000 per month you could invest a portion of your 401(k)s into an immediate annuity, which would supply lifetime income for both of you. If you invested $400,000 into an immediate annuity with a joint lifetime payout, you'd receive approximately $2,100 per month for the rest of both your lives. The remaining $200,000 in your 401(k)s can supply liquidity for emergency needs or be invested to grow in order to supply additional income in future years as inflation nibbles away at your purchasing power.

This is a simple solution that can solve one of the more vexing concerns of most retirees "running out of money." The downside of this solution is the money placed in the immediate annuity becomes illiquid. In most cases once you placed the money in this type of annuity and started the income stream, you can't change your mind. Therefore, I would only recommend considering this approach if you had a considerable sum of money that remained outside of the annuity in order to cover future spending needs and emergencies.

We briefly discussed the mechanics of Deferred Annuities in Chapter 2, these annuities come in two basic flavors variable or fixed.

An interesting feature has been added to many deferred annuities over the past decade.

Income guarantees.....

The income guarantee is a feature that allows the annuity to increase its income-paying ability by a fixed percentage annually, allowing the owner to defer taking income today in order to have higher income in the future.

Okay, that was a mouthful. Now let me explain it in plain English by using an example. Let's say you put $400,000 in a deferred annuity with a 7% income guarantee rider. Every year you defer taking income, the "income base" of $400,000 grows by 7% compounded; therefore the ability of your account to pay out higher income grows each year you don't take dollars out. In most cases the "income base growth rate" and the income "payout rate" can be different rates. For instance, the income base growth rate can be 7% and the income payout rate could be 5%.

I can see your head spinning, so here's another example.

Say you're 60 years old and planned on retiring at 65 with the same $400,000 as above. The chart below shows how the income guarantee would increase over time, providing increases in guaranteed income the longer you defer.

Figure 15

Years	Income Base-growth @7%	Income payout @5%	Account value
1	$428,000	$21,400	$400,000
2	$457,960	$22,898	?
3	$490,017	$24,500	?
4	$524,318	$26,166	?
5	$561,021	$28,051	?
10	$786,861	$39,343	?
15	$1,103,613	$55,180	?
20	$1,547,875	$77,394	?
25	$2,170,975	$108,549	?
30	$3,044,906	$152,245	?

Figure 15 clearly shows the longer you defer taking income, the higher it grows. The "income guarantee" provides you confidence in knowing exactly the amount of future income you'll receive and the peace of mind to know it is guaranteed for life.

The income guarantee is a contractual guarantee provided by the annuity company and cannot be changed by the company in the future. The income base will grow at the fixed rate (7%) regardless of interest rates, stock market fluctuations or economic changes.

Where else can you find an asset that can grow its income-producing ability consistently at 7% per year and payout sustainable income at 5%? I can't think of one, can you?

Keep in mind there are numerous annuity companies that provide income riders; while they're all similar, each have characteristics that make them unique. It's these characteristics that you must understand. Additionally, many income riders have a nominal cost associated with them. Make sure you ask your advisor to provide you with a list of all costs associated with your investments.

As I mentioned earlier, the predominant amount of business I did over the last 30 years has been with retirees and soon-to-be retirees. One of the primary focuses of my firm is designing and implementing retirement plans to produce income when it's required.

As you can imagine, using income guarantees can be very useful because they add the predictable results that most other assets cannot.

The 4% rule discussed earlier predicts the amount of income that can be withdrawn from a stock and bond portfolio. The primary reason the withdrawal rate is this low is because the assets (stocks and bonds) can change in value. The interest income generated by bonds can and do change, and as we all painfully know, stock prices are unpredictable. It is this volatility that causes the 4% withdrawal rate to be this low.

Annuities, especially fixed annuities, can provide a more generous income payout because principal values are fixed; they do not fluctuate as most other asset classes can.

Now that you understand the basics of how income guarantees work, I hope you can see how they can be a powerful retirement planning tool.

An important concept that you must understand before you invest money in an annuity with an income guarantee is that the "income base" and "account value" are two separate calculations.

Unfortunately, many individuals who now have income riders on their annuities don't understand this important distinction. I believe this is because most advisors that recommend them either don't understand the distinction themselves or do a poor job of explaining it to their clients.

In my example above, the *income base* grew at a fixed rate of 7%. The *account value* will grow at a rate based upon the underlying assets within the annuity. A *fixed annuity* may have an annual interest rate of 3% meaning the account value grows at 3% annually. In this case, the account value increases at a slower rate than the income base. A *variable annuity* that is made up mainly of mutual funds has direct market exposure; therefore, the account value may increase faster than the income base or it might decrease in value as the stock market falls.

I understand this is a bit confusing but once you comprehend the concept it makes perfect sense.

Back to Figure 15. Let's assume you're in a fixed annuity earning 3% annually; after 10 years, your *account value* would've grown from $400,000 to $537,566. In the same year the *income base* that is growing at 7% annually would have a value of $786,861.

If you owned a variable annuity, the *income base* would be exactly the same as the fixed annuity in this example. However, the account value may vary drastically. Because the variable annuities principle is not guaranteed, the initial investment of $400,000 could be worth more than the fixed annuity account value or it could actually lose money depending upon stock market volatility.

The "income base" is the value used to calculate your guaranteed income payments. The income base cannot be withdrawn in a lump sum. This is a common misunderstanding among investors. If you withdraw all funds from your account, the value you will receive will be the *account or cash value* not the income value or income base.

As I mentioned earlier, both variable and fixed annuities may come with income riders. While income riders on both types are very similar, the fixed annuity typically provides superior income guarantees. The reason for this is the variable annuity that is made up of mutual funds has market risk, while the fixed annuity does not. Similar to the 4% rule, it's the market volatility that causes the variable annuity to have an inferior income guarantee.

The income you receive stays consistent, regardless of the underlying growth rate of your account/annuity. Consider how a pension works. You're guaranteed a monthly income for life, regardless of how the assets within the pension are performing. The income guarantee acts in a similar fashion. Once you decide to start withdrawing income, the income amount is fixed. Therefore, your income stays consistent even if the growth rate of the assets falters.

Using Figure 15 as an example, if you started taking income in year 10, your income is guaranteed to be $39,343 annually for the rest of your life. This amount is exactly 5% of the income base. However, it will most likely be a different percentage of the account value. If the annuity averaged 3% per year as discussed above, the account value in year 10 would be

$537,566. Withdrawing 5% means you're pulling out more than your account is actually making, which means your account value will slowly decline. Let's do the math.

$537,566   beginning account value year 10
$16,127   3% fixed return-increase
$553,693   ending account value year 10
$39,343   guaranteed income value-withdrawn
$514,350   account value after income guarantee payout

As you can plainly see, the lifetime guaranteed income may be more than the growth rate of the account value, leading to a slow spend-down of the account value. While the withdrawal rate is precisely 5% of the income base, it is actually 7.11% of the account value ($39,343/$553,693). If this pattern continues long enough, you stand a chance of entirely depleting your account value.

This concept leads to one of the important features of the income guarantee. Remember I said earlier that the income is guaranteed for life. One of the features most income guarantees provide is to guarantee the income is for life, *even if the account value is entirely depleted*. Therefore, in the unlikely event you spend your account value down to $0, the income guarantee ($39,343) continues to be delivered to you for the remainder of your life.

Remember the "risk shifting" conversation from Chapter 1. Income guarantees can effectively shift the risk of running out of income from you and your spouse back on the shoulders of the annuity company.

Fixed Indexed Annuities

The Fixed Index Annuity is a cross between the fixed annuity and the variable annuity. As in a fixed annuity, the principal is guaranteed, and as in the variable annuity the return is based on a stock market index (commonly the S&P 500). Therefore, the FIA allows the investor to participate in the positive years of the stock market without fear of losing principal or past gains when the market declines. Additionally, many FIAs come with the ability to add an "income rider." This gives the FIA the unique ability to act as both a vehicle to provide long-term growth as well as predictable retirement income.

See the graph.

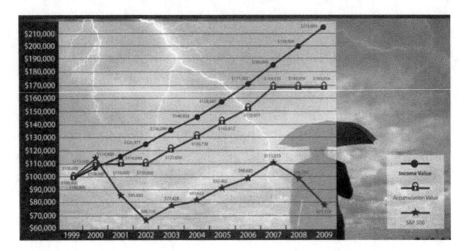

The account value (blue line) increases in value in the years the S&P 500 has positive gains, but does not lose value in the S&P 500 negative years (red line). The income base (black line) increases at a fixed annual return regardless of how the account value or S&P 500 performs.

Now to keep all the lawyers happy, this graph is used for example purposes only and should not be construed as predicting what will happen in the future. It should be used as an example of how the concept of the "Fixed Indexed Annuity" works.

Because the account value's growth is tied to a stock market index, we don't know what the *account value* will be worth in future years. However, what we do know is your principal and the past gains, which have been locked-in, cannot be lost because the market has a bad year. Additionally, the *income base* will continue to increase at its predetermined rate regardless of economic change, stock market volatility or interest rate swings.

FIAs can be an effective tool to *shift the risk* of the stock market from your assets back to the annuity company. Additionally, because of their principal guarantee they're less correlated to the stock market. Introducing the FIA into an investment portfolio or retirement account can enhance the risk-adjusted performance similar to that discussed in MPT earlier in this chapter.

Can you now see why the FIA has started to become an important piece of a well-designed retirement income plan? It's a financial tool that can allow your account value and future income to grow, without fear of negative events affecting you.

Life Insurance: The Best Deal in the Tax Code

It's not that I like life insurance; it's that I appreciate what it can do. It's no secret life insurance is a good deal for the beneficiaries, but the difficulty is explaining to a potential policy owner that they don't need to die in order to benefit.

Nationally recognized tax expert Ed Slott, CPA, was quoted in a recent TV appearance as saying, "The tax exemption for life insurance is the single biggest benefit in the tax code." The unfortunate truth is that most investors have no idea of the tax benefits, income options and growth potential that a properly designed life insurance policy allows.

We've discussed the tax benefits that life insurance contains in Chapter 2.

It's important to understand three primary factors that determine the growth of the cash value inside a life policy.

- How much money you invest or deposit
- Time
- Average annual rate of return

These three factors work together to determine how big your pile of money will be. And by extension, the size of your pile will determine the amount of income you can expect to receive.

These are the same factors that determine how big your 401(k), mutual fund, brokerage account or bank account will be.

To be fair, life insurance, as do all other types of investments, has costs. The primary cost to be concerned with in a life policy is the cost of insurance or COI. This is the cost to purchase the life insurance or death benefit attached to a policy. Depending on the type of policy you own there may be additional costs. It's important to understand all costs prior to purchasing or investing in any life policy. Minimizing these costs will allow the cash value to grow more efficiently.

Many different types of life insurance policies offer a myriad of different features, benefits and nuances. All life insurance policies have some of the same basic moving parts.

- Premiums: the amount you commit to pay for the policy
- Face amount or death benefit: the dollar amount beneficiaries will receive if you pass away (death benefits are income tax free)

As we discussed in Chapter 2, the concept of *over funding* is important to understand. The term *over funding* refers to the amount you invest or deposit in your insurance account over the COI. For example, if you purchase a policy with a $100,000 face amount, your COI might be $50 per month. Instead of sending the insurance company $50 premiums each month, you might send them $500 per month. The additional $450 is considered *over funding* and is placed in an investment account within the policy. Each month you send in your $500 premium, the investment account grows an additional $450 plus interest.

Most insurance companies shudder when you refer to life insurance or annuities as investments. However, I don't know another way to label an account where you place your money for the specific purpose of having it grow and fully expect to benefit from that growth at a later time.

Webster's Dictionary defines *investment* as the "outlay of money usually for income or profit; also the process of exchanging income for an asset that is expected to produce earnings at a later time."

I believe that anyone placing their hard-earned cash into life insurance or an annuity fully expects to reap a financial reward at some date in the future.

Consequently, we'll call it an investment even though the industry and its regulators frown on it.

In a Universal Life or Whole Life policy, the *cash value* created by the over funding typically earns an interest rate based on either:

- annual dividends (determined by the company)
- a fixed annual interest rate
- indexed interest rate (determined by a stock market index, similar to the FIA)

Because of the tax advantages mentioned in Chapter 2, the growth of the cash value is considered tax-deferred. And even better, when income is received from the policy it's tax-free.

Let me say that again... The income is tax-free!

To be accurate, when you receive income it is considered a loan against the death benefit of the policy. However, this loan never requires you to pay it back. If you understand how policy loans work, you'll truly recognize one of the enormous advantages offered within an insurance policy.

Loans from an insurance policy work differently than the typical loan. Most loans, of course, must be paid back over a period of time at a specified interest rate. Loans from retirement accounts such as 401(k)s and TSP accounts must be paid back within 5 years in order to avoid taxation on remaining loan balances. Any of you who've taken a loan from your retirement account already know the money you borrow comes directly from the investments within your retirement account. For example, if you have $300,000 in your 401(k) and wish to borrow $50,000 (maximum loan allowed by law, 72(p)(2)(D) IRC), your account balance is reduced to $250,000. This means you've borrowed your own money and it does not participate in any growth during the period the loan is outstanding.

Life insurance policy loans differ because you're not borrowing your own money; you are effectively borrowing money from the insurance company. Therefore, your cash remains firmly in your account receiving interest credits. There are typically two types of insurance policy loans, fixed and variable.

Fixed loans charge a fixed annual interest rate and variable loan rates fluctuate up or down depending on prevailing interest rates. Therefore the loan balance is constantly accruing based upon the current loan rate. However, all of your money stays invested within your policy earning interest.

Let's look at a quick example. Say you borrow $50,000 against your policy and the insurance company charges you a fixed rate of 4%. Annually the loan balance will accrue until the loan is paid off, approximately $2,000 annually, plus compounding.

Remember, you borrowed from the insurance company and not from your account. The $50,000 is still growing in your account. Let's assume you're using an indexing strategy (discussed below) that earned 6% during the policy year. The $50,000 would have generated $3,000 in gains during that particular year. Therefore, your loan balance would have increased $2,000 during that year, but your policy value will have increased $3,000 in that same year. Hence, because your borrowing costs were lower than your rate of return, your account or policy grew by that positive difference.

Of course, the opposite could happen. If the indexing strategy made less than the loan rate, the loan balance would grow faster than the growth within your policy. If your loan rate is 4% and your account grew 2%, the loan balance would grow faster than the policy value.

Most insurance companies offer a "wash loan." This is where companies will set their fixed loan rate at the same or approximately the same rate as their fixed interest account. Said another way, if the fixed loan rate is 4%, the interest rate on the fixed account within your policy will also be 4%, resulting in a "wash loan." The cost of the money you've borrowed and the return on the money you've made is equal; therefore, your cost for borrowing money is 0%. Because of this wash loan provision, fixed policy loans are considered more conservative.

A tactic to use in order to maximize the growth of your policy when you have a loan is to allocate an amount equal to your loan to the fixed interest strategy within your policy, leaving the balance of your policy invested in an indexing strategy, in order to allow for higher potential long-term returns.

I mentioned earlier that policy loans are not required to be paid back in the same fashion as loans against 401(k)s, TSPs and other retirement accounts. Policy loans accrue against the policy's death benefit value and are repaid at your eventual death. If the $50,000 loan discussed above eventually accrued to $100,000 at the time of your death, the amount paid to your heirs would be decreased by $100,000 in order to repay the insurance company. Keep in mind, because death benefits are income tax-free, the loan balance will be repaid with tax-free dollars.

Because policy loans are income tax free and do not require repayment, they make a very advantageous way to use an insurance policy as an effective retirement income tool.

In order to receive these wonderful tax benefits, the IRS spells out requirements you must abide by. The primary test the IRS requires is the "7 Pay Rule." This rule determines how much premium (money) that can be deposited inside the insurance policy for the first seven years. If the 7 Pay Rule is violated, the policy is deemed to be a MEC (Modified Endowment Contract), and causes any gains withdrawn from the policy to be subject to taxation and a 10% penalty if the policy owner is under 59 ½ years old.

Over the years, several insurance companies purposefully set out to design policies that enhance the growth of the cash value held within the policy for the purposes of income generation.

These policies strive to minimize the COI by holding the death benefit to the absolute minimum required to pass the 7 Pay Rule, thereby preserving its tax advantages. Additionally these policies attempt to enhance the growth rates of the cash value.

One of the more popular growth strategies is "indexing." We mentioned this briefly in Chapter 2. A policy's cash value is credited with an interest rate or growth rate determined by a stock market index, typically the S&P 500 or Dow Jones, although recently more indexes have been added. Similar to the FIAs we discussed earlier, the gains are determined by the stock market index without the fear of suffering losses in bad years.

This is much different than investing directly in the stock market, where you can make money or lose money, depending on market forces.

The index accounts within a life insurance policy differ from direct market exposure in two important ways. One difference is, if the stock market (S&P 500) increases during your account year, you typically don't receive all of the gains. Most policies have a "cap rate," which is the maximum gain you can receive in a particular year. Cap rates are currently around 12%, but can vary by company from 8 to 17%. Therefore, if your policy's cap rate is 15% and the S&P 500 increases 10%, your account is credited with 10% interest. On the other hand, if the S&P increases 20% your account would earn 15%, the cap rate.

The other important distinction of the index strategy is if the stock market falls in value during a particular year, you don't lose any money. Again, you're *shifting risk* away from you and back to the insurance company.

These indexing strategies allow the asset growth within insurance policies to be amplified by participating in the long-term growth the stock market provides, while protecting principal and past gains from deterioration caused by market setbacks.

Now let's look at how a properly designed life insurance account can be used to generate income.

Let's keep it simple: Steve is 50 and in good health and wants to invest $10,000 per year from now through 64. At that point he plans on retiring and will start using the money accumulated in his insurance policy as part of his retirement income solution.

In order to adhere to the 7 Pay Rule, the minimum amount of death benefit will be approximately $190,000. As the years go by, the death benefit will increase to approximately $400,000, because of the growth achieved within the policy.

If the growth of the assets within the policy can average 7% annually, the policy's value will be enough to supply Steve with over $19,000 per year from the age of 65 to 95.... And remember, the $19,000 is tax-free.

In simple terms, Steve invested $150,000 ($10,000 a year for 15 years) and withdrew and spent $589,000. When Steve dies he will have had income from his investment for 31 years, and his heirs will still receive an additional death benefit of around $110,000.

Let's Compare Apples to Oranges

I believe most of us plan on using our retirement plans in order to supplement our income after we retire. In most retirement plans, the investments and their growth are tax-deferred and the distribution or income is taxable.

Okay.... If an insurance policy can provide you $19,000 per year tax free, how much would you have to withdraw from your 401(k) to equal this amount?

Well, if you were in the 30% tax bracket, you have to withdraw $27,143 to equal the $19,000 tax-free provided by the insurance policy.

It would take $340,151 earning 7% annually to provide $27,143 per year for 31 years.

In order to save this $340,151 from age 50 through 64, you would have to invest $13,536 each year and earn about 7% annual return.

Which way is more efficient?

Saving $10,000 per year through your life insurance account or $13,536 in your 401(k)? You might be thinking that the 401(k) provides tax deductible contributions.

While this is true, let's look at it using real dollars. If you were in the 30% income tax bracket, the tax savings on the 401(k) contribution would amount to $4,060. Eureka. The after-tax cost of the 401(k) contribution is $9,475. Therefore, it's more efficient to invest your money in a 401(k) than a life insurance policy.

Now let's take it a step further. By investing in a 401(k), you saved $60,900 in taxes ($4,060 for 15 years). When you start withdrawing the $27,143 annually at retirement, you'll pay $8,143 in taxes (30%) leaving you with $19,000 to spend. Another way to look at it is that it took you 15 years to save $60,900 in taxes by contributing to the 401(k). When you started taking income from the 401(k), it took you 7.5 years to pay back all the taxes it took you 15 years to save. Chances are, you'll pay substantially more income taxes taking income from your 401(k) than you saved by contributing to it. Additionally if taxes were to increase in the future the income advantage of the life insurance policy would be magnified.

You might be scratching your head and thinking..... both investments are equal, one doesn't have an advantage over the other.

Well, if everything worked exactly as described above you're right – they'd be equal.

The life policy can provide other benefits that should be considered. What if things changed from age 50 through 95 then which investment are you most comfortable with?

What if:

- you passed away unexpectedly prior to retirement
- the stock market was volatile over the remainder of your lifetime
- you had unexpected emergencies and needed to use part of your savings
- taxes didn't stay at 30%, but increased

I think you agree that any of these items could easily happen. And if one or more did, the life insurance investment would most likely be most effective. Let me explain.

- If you die prematurely, you'll most likely not have had enough time to save adequately within your 401(k). The same could be said for the life insurance policy; however, it has a death benefit that acts as a "self completing" failsafe. Therefore, if you pass away prematurely the insurance policy would provide adequate funds to supply the necessary income for your family.

- Over the last 80 years there have been 15 bear markets, instances where the stock market fell 20% or more. What are the chances this could happen again over a 31-year retirement? The answer is 100%. The real question is how many bear markets will you see while you're retired. If you remember, we discussed in Chapter 2 that when using your retirement accounts to provide income, the *sequence of returns* is what's important. Stock market volatility combined with income can cause assets to be spent down prematurely. Because the insurance policy uses the "index strategies" that prevent market losses, the probability of account spend down is greatly diminished.

- Life happens. What are the chances you may need to unexpectedly pull money from your retirement accounts? If you pull money from your 401(k), you will be taxed and penalized (pre-59 ½). With the insurance account, money can be withdrawn without taxes or penalties (policy loan). If you borrow money from your 401(k), you must pay it back within five years. If you borrow money from your insurance account, you're under no obligation to pay it back. The

IRS considers the loan as a loan against the death benefit. The loan is repaid when you pass away.

- Do you think tax rates will increase or decrease in the future? While, I don't have a crystal ball, it appears to be evident taxes will increase in the future. If you receive a tax savings of 30% when you contribute to your 401(k) and subsequently pay a higher tax rate when you take income distribution at retirement, then it wouldn't make economic sense to defer taxes.

Let's change the above example. Instead of being taxed 30% on the $27,143 withdrawn from your 401(k) at age 65, you instead were taxed at a higher rate of 35%. The $9,500 of tax would cause your spendable income to fall to $17,643. This makes the cash flow from the 401(k) inferior to the $19,000 from the insurance policy.

After reading this, you may think that I believe life insurance is the best thing since sliced bread. It may surprise you to find out that I don't. I do, however, believe that in the right circumstances life insurance can provide benefits beyond other forms of investment.

Used properly, a life insurance policy can be an effective financial tool. It can be used for asset accumulation as well as an effective way to distribute tax advantaged income, not to mention offer insurance protection to your family.

Designing a policy correctly is a task most financial advisors don't understand. Many will downplay its benefits because they either don't comprehend them or they want to sell you something else.

In order to determine if an insurance policy can assist you in achieving your financial goals, you must find a competent financial advisor with the experience and understanding of the intricacies of life insurance.

"Move your money from accounts that are forever taxed to accounts that are never taxed."

–Ed Slott, CPA

Social Security: Not As Simple As You Think

Until the past couple of years, Social Security was almost an afterthought when it came to income planning. It took the Great Recession of 2008-2009 to push Social Security back into the limelight. When retirement account balances were cut in half and job security became uncertain, the relevance of Social Security income as an important future income stream gained attention. Future recipients are just now starting to take Social Security seriously.

Most individuals today will retire with multiple income streams. Social Security will likely be one of those streams. However, when considering the best time to initiate Social Security benefits, most people simply start the payments without much thought.

Depending on which source you read, approximately 85% of the Social Security recipients start their benefits early, at age 62. It's common knowledge that Full Retirement Age (FRA) is somewhere between 65 and 67 years old, depending on when you were born. Taking benefits earlier then FRA causes Social Security benefits to be reduced. If you start at age 62, your benefits are reduced to 75% of what they would have been had you taken them at your FRA. However, if you wait until after FRA to qualify for Delayed Retirement Credits or DRCs, this will cause your benefits to increase by approximately 8% for every year you wait, until age 70. Here's an example.

Let's say you're 62 and you plan on retiring. You look at this year's Social Security statement and it tells you:

- benefits at age 62 will be $1,845 per month
- benefits at age 66 (FRA) will be $2,460 per month ($2,794 after inflation allowances)
- benefits at age 70 will be $3,247 per month ($4,050 after inflation allowances)

You can plainly see that the longer you wait to begin your monthly paychecks, the bigger they'll be. In looking at these figures, it's hard to understand why most recipients elect to take income as soon as they are eligible. Perhaps they need the extra income or they believe their life expectancy is less than average; therefore, starting sooner will net more money over their shortened lifetime. While these are both plausible reasons, I can't help but believe the primary reason is, they don't know their alternatives.

If you consider the amount of additional income you'll receive by waiting a few short years, it might surprise you. Let's look at the situation in Figure 16, on the next page, assuming your life expectancy is 80 years and the Cost of Living Allowance (COLA) is 2.8%. Figure 16 show the differential in lifetime aggregate income between claiming early benefits at 62 versus either waiting until FRA at 66 or DRC at age 70 is $545,539, $604,185 and $616,197 respectively.

The difference becomes even larger ($743,388, $876,954 and $964,312 respectively) if you assume a life expectancy of 85 years.

The difference between starting early, versus delaying benefits, can mean a difference of over $220,000 or almost 30% more income over your life expectancy. Are you starting to see why choosing the right Social Security strategy is an important part of your overall retirement income plan?

What's equally striking is the monthly income differential. Using Figure 16, at age 80, annual income would be: $36,396, $48,523 or $64,057 respectively.

If you wait to start benefits at age 70 instead of 62 the annual income when you reach 80 is $64,057 and $36,390 respectively, a 76% difference.

Figure 16

Bob, Betty and Bill, each 62 now, all live to age 80

Age	Year	Bob's Annual Benefit With 2.8% COLAs	Cumulative total	Betty's Annual Benefit With 2.8% COLAs	Cumulative total	Bill's Annual Benefit With 2.8% COLAs	Cumulative total
62	2012	$21,140	$21,140	$0	$0	$0	$0
63	2013	$22,760	$44,900	$0	$0	$0	$0
64	2014	$23,397	$68,297	$0	$0	$0	$0
65	2015	$24,052	$92,349	$0	$0	$0	$0
66	2016	$24,726	$117,075	$32,964	$32,964	$0	$0
67	2017	$25,418	$142,493	$33,887	$66,851	$0	$0
68	2018	$26,130	$168,623	$34,836	$101,687	$0	$0
69	2019	$26,861	$195,485	$35,811	$137,498	$0	$0
70	2020	$27,614	$223,098	$36,814	$174,312	$48,600	$48,600
71	2021	$28,387	$251,485	$37,845	$212,157	$49,961	$98,561
72	2022	$29,182	$280,666	$38,904	$251,061	$51,360	$149,921
73	2023	$29,999	$310,665	$39,994	$291,055	$52,798	$202,718
74	2024	$30,839	$341,504	$41,114	$332,168	$54,276	$256,994
75	2025	$31,702	$373,206	$42,265	$374,433	$55,796	$312,790
76	2026	$32,590	$405,796	$43,448	$417,881	$57,358	$370,148
77	2027	$33,502	$439,298	$44,665	$462,546	$58,964	$429,113
78	2028	$34,440	$473,738	$45,915	$508,461	$60,615	$489,728
79	2029	$35,405	$509,143	$47,201	$555,662	$62,312	$552,040
80	2030	$36,396	$545,539	$48,523	$604,185	$64,057	$616,097
81	2031	$37,415	$582,954	$49,881	$654,066	$65,851	$681,948
82	2032	$38,463	$621,417	$51,278	$705,344	$67,695	$749,642
83	2033	$39,540	$660,956	$52,714	$758,057	$69,590	$819,232
84	2034	$40,647	$701,603	$54,190	$812,247	$71,539	$890,771
85	2035	$41,785	$743,388	$55,707	$867,954	$73,542	$964,312

You're probably thinking, if I started taking benefits early how long would it take me to break even if I waited until age 66 or even age 70? Using the data and Figure 16, break even is:

Benefit start ages	62 versus 66	66 versus 70	62 versus 70
Breakeven age	78	80	78

Therefore, the important question is "what is your life expectancy?" If you consider your family history as well as your own physical condition, this might give you an idea of your life expectancy under normal circumstances. It's no secret that life expectancy has increased from generation to generation. According to Social Security life expectancy tables, the life expectancy for a male aged 60 is approximately 82 and for a female, 84. This means on average, 50% of the 60-year-old men and women will pass away prior to ages 82 and 84; however, the other 50% will live longer. The real question is which side of the fence you fall on.

Another consideration to keep in mind is that if you're married, your spouse will inherit your Social Security benefits after your death (assuming your Social Security benefits are higher than that of your surviving spouse). Therefore, if one of your income planning goals is to make sure your spouse will have adequate income after your death, delaying Social Security benefits may help in providing that additional income. For example, using the data in Figure 16, the difference in income can be striking. If you started benefits early at 62 versus age 70 and subsequently died at age 85, the annual income your surviving spouse would inherit would be $41,785 versus $73,541, a 76% difference.

Many married couples will accrue separate Social Security benefits that they can claim independently in order to maximize the overall income benefit. Many individuals are unaware that Social Security spousal benefits can be claimed in lieu of individual benefits. Keep in mind that spousal benefits are 50% of your FRA benefit amount.

Let's set up an example to describe some of the little-known claiming strategies:

- Bob and Sally both turned 66 the same year (full retirement age).
- Bob's Social Security is $2,200 per month and Sally's is $800 per month.
- Cost-of-living allowance of 2.8% (COLA).

I don't mean to be chauvinistic but because of raising children, women many times spend fewer years in the workforce, thereby accruing smaller Social Security benefits. I realize this isn't always the case, but it can help display some of the tactics and strategies that can be used between spouses to maximize overall income benefits.

In the above example, Bob and Sally could file and claim their own individual Social Security benefits ($2,200 and $800 respectively). Or Sally can claim spousal benefits against Bob's Social Security benefits equaling $1,100. In this basic example the answer is obvious.

However, Bob and Sally could consider alternatives.

Alternative 1: *File and Suspend*

In this technique the higher income earning spouse (Bob) starts taking his benefits at Full Retirement Age (FRA) and Sally claims spousal benefits of $1,100. Bob then suspends (stops) his benefits and allows them to accrue in order to receive higher DRC at age 70. At that point, Bob's Social Security would increase to approximately $2,904 monthly (plus COLAs).

This allows Sally to start claiming spousal benefits while Bob's benefits continue to accrue to be tapped later. Sally has access to an additional $1,100 per month, which can be used to pay down debts, add to retirement savings or be spent enjoying life.

The "File and Suspend" strategy may be attractive to a couple whose main breadwinner would like to continue to work past FRA.

Alternative 2: *File and Switch*

In this strategy, the lower earning spouse files for their own benefits early, at age 62. Upon the retirement of the higher income spouse, the lower income spouse switches to spousal benefits (assuming they're higher).

In our example, Sally starts her own Social Security benefits at age 62. Because she is taking benefits early, they'll be reduced from $800 per month to approximately $620. Bob continues to work until full retirement age (FRA) of 66 before starting benefits of $2,200 per month. At that point, Sally switches from her own benefits to spousal benefits of $1,100 per month.

This strategy allows Sally to receive an additional $620 per month from age 62 through 66 when she expects to switch spousal benefits based on Bob's earnings record. The strategy should only be used if spousal benefits are expected to be higher than benefits at FRA. In this example, Sally's benefits at FRA are $800 per month versus spousal benefits of $1100 per month, making the strategy valid.

Alternative 3: *Withdraw Now and Withdraw More Later*

In this tactic, the lower income earning spouse applies for benefits early at age 62. The higher income earning spouse at 66 (FRA) claims spousal benefits against the lower earning spouses benefits. The higher income spouse allows their own benefits to accrue to be applied for at age 70.

Sally applies for early benefits at age 62, $620 per month. At FRA of 66, Bob applies for spousal benefits against Sally's Social Security. This will yield Bob approximately $340 per month in spousal benefits. Bob allows his own benefits to receive DRC until age 70, where his benefits will increase from $2,200 to $2,904 monthly.

The strategy allows Bob and Sally to claim Social Security benefits of approximately $980 per month ($620 for Sally plus $340 for Bob) while allowing Bob to delay taking his Social Security in order to maximize its benefit.

These three Social Security alternative claiming strategies are just a few of many that can be used in order to optimize Social Security income. The one that works best for you depends on your individual circumstances. Also keep in mind that most claiming strategies require one or both spouses to be at full retirement age.

Just in case you were wondering which strategy would optimize Bob and Sally's Social Security income? Here goes...

- Sally begins to take benefits of $800 per month based on her own earnings record at age 66.
- Bob files for spousal benefits of $400 per month at age 66 based on Sally's earnings history.
- At age 70, Bob switches to benefits of $2,904 monthly based on his own earnings record.

- Sally, at age 70, switches to spousal benefits of $1,100 per month. This benefit is calculated based on Bob's FRA amount not his DRC at 70.
- At Bob's death (assumed 85 years), Sally will receive survivor benefits of $2,904 per month ($5478 after COLA).

It should be noted that all of the data listed above will increase annually based upon COLAs. In order to keep these examples easy to follow, I did not include those adjustments, therefore these numbers are understated.

If both Bob and Sally live to their assumed life expectancies of 85 and 90 respectively, their aggregate income from Social Security benefits will be $1,516,125.

Divorced and Widowed Spouse Benefits

If you have been divorced or widowed, you may still be eligible for Social Security benefits based on your ex- or late spouse's Social Security benefits.

If you are married for at least 10 years and have been divorced for at least 2 years and are 62, you'll qualify for benefits based on your ex-spouse's work history. You can apply for these benefits even if your ex-spouse has not applied for his or her own benefits. If you remarry the benefits will stop.

Get this, if you have more than one ex-spouse that fits the above description you may claim benefits based on the higher earning ex-spouse. You may even be eligible if your ex-spouse passes away.

There are claiming strategies that can be used to maximize your Social Security benefits utilizing your ex-spouse's benefits, similar to the ones described above.

If your spouse has passed away, you're still eligible to claim benefits based on his or her earnings history. A widow or widower is entitled to the higher earner's retirement benefit. In other words, if your deceased spouse's Social Security benefits would have been higher than yours, you're entitled to their higher benefit amount. Additionally, you can begin these benefits as early as age 60. It should be noted that if you do start receiving these benefits early, they'll be reduced.

If you have a child under the age of 16 or who is disabled, you may be eligible to start benefits immediately, even if you're under the age of 60. As with divorces, if you remarry, the benefits stop. However, the Social Security Administration gives widows and widowers a break on the remarriage rule. If you remarry after the age of 60, the income benefits will continue.

Social Security will more than likely be one of several income streams that you'll depend upon in retirement. I hope you now understand how important using the right strategy can be when claiming your benefits.

Keep Your Income Tax Efficient

In thinking about retirement planning, most investors spend most of this time pondering the most appropriate investment choices to make within their plans. Few give much thought to planning how the income can be generated by these plans, much less considering the effect taxes can have on this future income.

In past generations most retirees receive their income from typically two sources: their company pension and Social Security. Future generations will most likely have multiple sources of income in retirement. These sources of income all have different tax implications in your overall income picture. They should be considered individually and collectively when putting together a retirement income strategy.

When reading this section, keep in mind that there isn't *one best way* to create a retirement income strategy. The one that will work most effectively for you depends upon your unique characteristics and needs. What I hope to do is to show that there is more than one way to *skin the cat* and try to get you to think past the obvious.

For most of us, receiving either Social Security and/or a pension will provide a substantial part of our retirement income. Maximizing these cash flows is extremely important; however, the purpose of this section is to discuss how other sources of income such as dividends, capital gains and retirement plan distributions can be combined most *effectively* with primary income sources such as Social Security and pension income.

It goes without saying that maximizing the amount of income provided by all sources is important, but considering how these income sources will be taxed is something that deserves equal care.

Both pension and Social Security income are taxed as ordinary income. If and when you receive these sources of income, there is not much you can do to alter how they're taxed. But planning how you receive income from other sources at your disposal can reduce your overall tax exposure, thereby leaving you more money to spend on lifestyle.

Most retirement savers as well as their advisors, whether they know it or not, formulate some sort of strategy when planning for retirement income. Most of strategies fall into one of four types:

1. No strategy
2. Systematic withdrawal
3. Bucket income strategy
4. Tax efficient bucket income strategy

No Strategy: Many investors and their advisors spend little time working on overall income plans. Most of their efforts are spent on investing and growing various buckets of money, such as retirement accounts and investment portfolios. Not much thought is given to how these buckets of assets can be used to supply income in the future.

Systematic withdrawal: This strategy is popular amongst individuals who use stock, mutual funds and exchange traded funds (ETF) as the primary investment vehicles within their retirement plans. When the investor/retiree decides to start withdrawing money from their various investment plans, they *systematically* sell shares in order to provide a desired monthly or quarterly cash flow. This plan works well as long as markets continually increase and the timeframe that you'll need your income is relatively short. But, as we discussed numerous times throughout this book, investment markets don't continually rise and life expectancies are steadily increasing. This combination can be deadly for an investment portfolio's ability to provide long-term income... Remember the 4% rule.

Bucket income strategy: This strategy is typically introduced to investors by advisors who have experience in income planning. The idea is to create separate buckets of income that will supplement pension and Social Security income. Let's say your pension and Social Security income is $4,000 per month and your total income need is $7,000 per month. Your investment and retirement portfolios need to produce $3,000 per month or $36,000 annually.

A simple bucket strategy would be to allocate enough money to an investment that will consistently provide $3,000 per month. Annuities can work well as the investment vehicle for this bucket. In a typical bucket strategy, two or three buckets of income are created as a supplement to Social Security and pensions. If done properly, these buckets can also provide additional income to help offset the effects of inflation. Figure 17 shows an example of a three-bucket strategy.

Bucket number 1 is funded with short-term investments designed to provide the required income ($3,000) for the first five retirement years. At that point bucket 2 kicks in, which is funded with conservative investments designed to grow for five years and then supply income for the next 10 plus years. After year 15, the long-term growth investments in bucket 3 will start providing additional income to supplement other retirement income along with bucket 2 income. Each phase or bucket of income should be designed to provide an increase in income in order to counter inflation.

There are countless different variations off of this strategy. If you're reading this book in a coffeehouse, look around at the other people sipping on their morning Joe. Not one person there will have a strategy just like yours. You're unique, and so is your income plan.

Figure 17

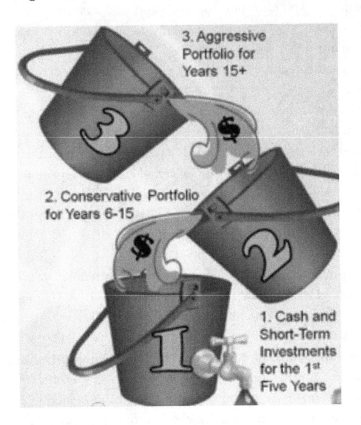

Tax Efficient Bucket Income Strategy: This strategy takes the "bucket income strategy" to the next level. All income sources are analyzed for their tax efficiency as it pertains to supplying you with the required income. The idea is to provide you with the income you'll require and control your income tax liability simultaneously.

As Figure 18 displays, income from various sources will be taxed at different rates. The trick is to provide you with the income you want, while controlling the tax bite on that income. This is best done by creating sources of income with tax advantages.

Let's use the same example as above. Your income from Social Security and pension is $4,000 per month, and falls within the "ordinary income" bucket. If you refer back to the 2013 tax brackets in Chapter 1, you'll see this falls in the 15% Married Filing Jointly Federal income tax bracket. The key here is to receive the additional $3,000 per month you require without increasing your tax bracket. Referring to the Tax Brackets in Chapter 1, you'll see you that adjusted gross income (AGI) up to $72,500 is taxed at the 15% bracket. Therefore, if your income requirements are $7,000 per month or $84,000 annually, the amount over $72,500 ($11,500) will be taxed at the higher 25% bracket.

If your annual Social Security and pension income is $48,000, you've got room for another $24,500 of income before you're pushed into a higher tax bracket.

To be more precise, only up to 85% of your Social Security income is taxed at a Federal level and many States will not tax it either. However, in order to keep this example user friendly I didn't include these within the calculation.

Okay, let's see if we can keep you within the 15% tax bracket. Your ordinary income from Social Security and pension is $48,000 per year. Unless you decide to defer your pension or Social Security income, it will be taxed as ordinary income. While there are advanced strategies that involve deferring Social Security and/or pension income, for the purposes of this exercise we'll assume you will receive these sources of income as part of your annual income.

You need to find $3,000 per month from the Long-Term Capital Gain, Tax-Deferred Ordinary Income or Tax-Free Buckets. There are various ways this puzzle can be solved.

1. Withdraw up to $24,500 from your IRAs or 401(k)s in the tax-deferred ordinary income bucket and withdraw the remaining $11,500 from your tax-free bonds, life insurance or Roth accounts.

2. Assuming you have substantial assets in nonqualified stocks and mutual funds in the Long-Term Capital Gains bucket, you may sell shares to create the additional $36,000 you'll need to support your lifestyle. If you're married filing jointly and your adjusted gross income is under $250,000 ($200,000 single filer), all capital gains and dividend income is taxed at the 15% bracket (2013 tax year).

3. If you have substantial assets that fall into the Tax-Free bucket, you may utilize these in order to supply the additional $36,000 required. The strategy might be used in order to allow the assets in the Tax-Deferred bucket to continue growing until age 70 ½, at which time Required Minimum Distribution rules will cause forced withdrawals. RMDs will be taxed as ordinary income; therefore if RMDs don't provide the additional income required, funds can be withdrawn from either the Long-Term Capital Gain or Tax-Free bucket to round off the additional income.

4. Use the difference between your current AGI and the next tax bracket as a way to convert Traditional retirement accounts into Roth accounts. For example, if your current AGI is $80,000, you are firmly in the 25% federal income tax bracket. However, the top end of the 25% bracket is $146,400. Therefore you can convert up to $66,400 from your traditional retirement accounts into a Roth account without leaving the 25% tax bracket.

Granted, this will cause additional taxation; however, the converted assets would have been taxed eventually and possibly at a higher rate, perhaps making this a wise decision.

As you can see there are many different combinations to control your taxes while supplying you with the required income to meet your lifestyle. The trick is to have the foresight and the appropriate financial advice to establish these various buckets of money in advance of the time you'll need them.

Figure 18

Andy Barkate

2013 Tax Rates

Ordinary Income	Capital Gains Income	Tax Deferred Income	Tax Free Income
Pension Income	Stock & Bond	IRA	Municipal Bonds
Interest Income	Exchange Traded Funds	401k/TSP	Roth IRA/401k
Earned Income-W-2	Mutual Funds	Annuities	Life Insurance
Corporate & Government Bonds	Real Estate-REITS		
Passive Income	Qualified Dividends		
Tax Rate 10-39.6%	0-15%	10-39.6%	0%

*A 3.8% Medicare Surtax on Net Investment Income (Capital Gains) for those Individual and Joint filers over $200,000 and $250,000 respectively will apply

Fees and Costs: The Higher the Cost, the Lower Your Income

I don't need to tell you that all investments come with fees and costs. Understanding the costs you're paying and determining if they are reasonable is obviously important. It's not hard to comprehend that a higher fee will result in money you would have ordinarily earned going into someone else's pocket.

However, many individuals believe their investments have low fees and in some cases, no fees, and many others have no clue what the fees lie within their investment products.

Mutual funds are one of the mainstays in most investment and retirement plans. In an April 4, 2011, *Forbes* article entitled *"The Real Cost of Owning a Mutual Fund,"* author Ty A. Bernicke discussed costs associated with owning mutual funds. The cost that most of us know is the *management fee* or *expense ratio*. Bernicke also discussed costs that elude the average investor such as transaction costs, cash drag and tax costs.

According to Bernicke, the expense ratio of the average stock mutual fund is .90%, which on the surface seems relatively tame. However, consider the average transaction costs of 1.44%, cash drag of .83% and average tax costs of around 1.00%.

Transaction costs are the costs associated with buying and selling securities within the mutual funds portfolio. They can be difficult to find because in most cases they are not disclosed in the fund's prospectus.

Cash drag is the cost associated with a fund holding cash. All funds hold a certain amount of their assets in cash, primarily for investor redemption purposes. Percentage returns on cash holdings are typically far less than gains on the investment portfolios held by a mutual fund. Additionally, an investor is paying the *expense ratio* on all of the assets held in the fund, not just the money actually invested. Therefore, investors are paying management fees on money (cash) that is not actually invested.

Tax costs are the drag on a mutual fund's portfolio created by paying taxes on capital gains, dividends and interest generated annually by the investment portfolios. While retirement accounts such as 401(k)s, TSPs and IRAs aren't affected by annual tax costs, you will pay taxes when you decide to withdraw the money from these accounts. As discussed in Chapter 2, capital gains and dividends typically offer preferential tax treatment, but when they are distributed from a retirement account, they're taxed at higher ordinary income tax rates. This is a good point to keep in mind when you're considering which types of assets to hold inside and outside of your retirement accounts.

Please note: These are *average* fund costs, meaning half of mutual funds will have either higher or lower cost structures.

Managed or Wrap Accounts

Managed or wrap accounts are arrangements where individual investment accounts are personally managed by professional money managers. The idea here is the investor will receive more individual consideration as to the types of securities held within their account and perhaps a heightened awareness of market conditions and their effects on these securities.

Of course, these accounts come with their own management fees, which can typically range from .50% to 2.50% annually. Managed accounts can hold a variety of different securities ranging from stocks, bonds, ETFs, cash, REITs and mutual funds. Managed accounts started to gain popularity with major brokerage firms in the 1990s because of the ability to generate ongoing revenue streams for the brokerage firm. Today, managed accounts comprise a large percentage, if not the majority, of the income generated by most brokerage firms.

Over the past dozen years, I've run across countless individuals who've had managed accounts at the major and regional brokerage firms. What I noticed in the majority of these accounts was that a large percentage of the assets are made up of mutual funds. It doesn't take a rocket scientist to do the math on the annual fees. When you combine the fees charged by the managed account with the fees and charges within mutual funds, total fees could easily range from 3 to 4% annually. This level of cost is hard to justify.

You might find it odd if I told you I liked managed accounts... the fact is, I do.

Managed accounts can offer an individual investor a level of investment sophistication that they might not be able to replicate themselves. Fees and costs should be scrutinized because they're not only a drag on positive returns and annual income, but they will exaggerate account losses.

I don't mean to beat up on mutual funds and managed accounts, but because many retirement-minded investors use these types of accounts as their primary investment vehicles, they should bear heightened scrutiny.

As I've mentioned numerous times throughout this book, my goal is to discuss methods to grow your retirement assets in such a way that they will produce sustainable and consistent income throughout retirement. Additionally, as I discussed in detail in this chapter as well as in Chapter 2, relying on volatile assets (stocks bonds and mutual funds) as the primary source of continuous income is problematic. When you attach the burden of costs and fees to asset volatility, it makes their ability to produce sustainable income that much more difficult.

All investments have some sort of fee or cost attached to them. Fixed annuities will pay a fixed return, but rest assured the insurance company is making a spread over and above the return you're receiving. This "spread" should be viewed as a cost. Bank Money Market Accounts and CDs operate much the same way. In life insurance, the cost of insurance or COI is a drag on the tax-free investment returns we discussed earlier in this chapter.

To better illustrate the effect costs and fees can have on long-term asset growth, consider the graph in Figure 19. The chart illustrates the relationship between *fees* and *time*, which is important to understand. It's intuitive that higher fees will result in decreased account growth, but as the graph indicates how the introduction of *time* greatly exaggerates this effect.

The 30-year time horizon used in Figure 19 is appropriate because many of us will rely on our retirement accounts to produce income for extended periods of time, which could easily be 30 years or longer.

As you can see the difference between the accounts that had a cost of 1, 2 and 3% is approximately $1.9 to $3.2 million. Granted, that is over 30 years, but wouldn't you rather have the money paid in fees to spend on you and your lifestyle?

Figure 19

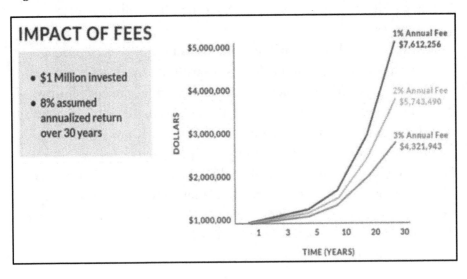

I understand that not everyone has $1 million floating around, but the importance of reducing unnecessary costs is key no matter what the size of your account.

Putting It All Together

The idea of this chapter is to show how a retirement income plan should be put together, starting with:

- Investment Policy Statement or IPS
- Income needed
- Income sources
- Assets
- Debts and liabilities
- Future changes to expenses and income
- Considering tax changes and inflation
- Factor market volatility to show why you want to minimize the use of stocks
- Have a plan to build wealth...not chase it

I debated for some time on how to approach this section of the book, or if I wanted to omit the ideas in this section entirely. Putting together a workable retirement and income plan is an extremely individual undertaking. Every one of you reading this book will have a different "best plan." Additionally, there's not a universal "playbook" on how to create the optimum plan. Each individual has different likes and dislikes, risk tolerance, time horizon, tax exposure, past experiences and expectations of the future. Each of us will have events in our lives and the lives of our families that will make our needs unique to us and us alone. Therefore, your retirement plan should be unique.

Investment Policy Statement

By failing to prepare, you are preparing to fail.
–Benjamin Franklin

The IPS or Investment Policy Statement is a document detailing the relationship between a financial adviser and their clients. Smart investors know, of course, that they should stick to an investment plan and modify it only when their personal circumstances change, not on market fluctuations or knee-jerk reactions. But that's easier said than done. One technique that can help is the implementation of an IPS.

An IPS is a *written* document that articulates the investor's overall investment goals and how those goals will be accomplished. It's designed to take the emotion out of the investing process and keep the investor on track, regardless of what the market or the economy is doing. Investors can write an IPS on their own or with professional help.

I'm willing to bet that most people who read this book have at one time or another thought about compiling an IPS. However, I'm also willing to bet that about 95% of you haven't. An IPS should be a detailed plan, not a general statement. It should cover such specifics as investment objectives, desired annual returns, asset allocation, tax management strategies, benchmarks, rebalancing methods and monitoring procedures.

Start by identifying your investment goals: college, retirement, legacy planning or charitable intent. How much should be set aside in cash reserves? Will you be making withdrawals down the road such as purchasing a car, paying for weddings or college educations?

Once you know where you're going and your investment needs, you can determine what savings rate and rates of return are required to accomplish that goal. Remember, a retirement plan is not designed to simply make as much money as possible. It's designed to accomplish specific goals. That's where the IPS is able to restrain investors from overreaching or panicking. For example, if the IPS determines that an earning rate of 6 percent annually is sufficient to accomplish your goals, you'll be less tempted to jump on a highflying stock just because it might earn 50% percent or, consequently, lose 50%.

Does the investment risk you're willing to take (really defined as *how much money you can stomach losing*) match your goals? Say you want or need that 6% return to accomplish your goals, but you don't want to invest in anything except CDs and short-term bonds. Historically, these types of investments have not provided that level of return over the long run, whereas stocks may. Consequently, you'll have to either adjust your goals or your risk tolerance.

What role will taxes play in your plan? Do you want to harvest tax losses in order to minimize tax gains, or will you be invested primarily in tax-favored accounts? What is your investment time horizon—retirement in 15 years or college for Junior in 10? All these factors need to be incorporated into the IPS.

Now it's time for the IPS to identify what asset classes and investment vehicles are most appropriate for your needs. Here you may want to prescribe certain limits. For example, no more than 50 % in equities (stocks), with that percentage broken down by large cap, small cap, international, real estate and so on; 35 % in bonds; and 15 % in cash. You might want the IPS to specifically state that you will not invest in certain types of investments, such as initial public offerings, junk bonds or commodities.

If you plan to use mutual funds, state whether you want to use primarily index funds, more actively managed funds, or a combination. Do you plan to pick individual stocks? Do you prefer growth or value stocks? Do you prefer government or corporate bonds?

Just the act of writing down these issues and factors forces you to clearly think out your investment strategies and stay on track, versus floating along with no particular plan, which is what most investors do. Although a written document, an IPS is not carved in stone. You can revise it when appropriate. In the meantime, it will see you through volatile times and minimize those swings caused by greed and fear.

Write it Down

"If you don't know where you are going, you'll end up someplace else."
— Yogi Berra

Having a written plan on describing how you'll get from point A to point B is essential. This may seem like common sense, but according to a 2012 study done by the Certified Financial Planner Board of Standards, only 31% of American families have actually done this.

There's something about committing your ideas and goals into written form. It seems to make them more tangible and give them more meaning. It also provides a point of reference to gauge your progress. Similar to the IPS, a well-structured retirement plan document can help guide you in times of uncertainty and keep you moving forward in the right direction.

There are countless online calculators to help you determine if you're saving enough to fund your retirement income needs. While these can give you a good idea of how much money you'll need to save and which level of return you must achieve to meet your goals, they fall short in actually providing an all-encompassing, workable solution to your individual needs..... which is your "Retirement Plan."

Many retirement-minded individuals make the mistake of confusing investment planning with retirement planning. In the broad sense, an investment plan is a subset of the retirement or financial plan. The IPS is an essential part of a well-thought-out investment plan, which in turn is part of a well-designed retirement plan.

An investment plan will help you accumulate the assets you'll need to supply the supplementary income that will last throughout retirement. As discussed above, the IPS can encompass many types of investment areas.

In the end, the retirement plan is an income plan. It should cover income for both you and your surviving spouse as well as provide for the smooth transfer of your assets to heirs after you pass. It should cover all of the elements that must come together in order for you to retire in the style you wish. Not only should it detail your investment strategies and the various income streams you will receive in retirement, it should also discuss areas such as debt reduction, tax strategy, inflation protection and unforeseen financial speed bumps such as medical issues and premature death.

Investment Planning v. Income Planning

Unfortunately, most people believe that investment planning is synonymous with retirement planning. After all, you're saving and investing with the idea of accumulating a nest egg for retirement. However, the mindset between the two is drastically different. As we've discussed numerous times in this book, the assets that one accumulates within their retirement accounts will most probably be used to subsidize their lifestyle throughout retirement. Therefore, somewhere along the line a plan designed to grow your assets becomes a plan to distribute those assets in the form of income. This is where the mindset between investment planning and retirement planning becomes more obvious.

The timing is different for all of us, but there comes an age where we can truly visualize retiring. Hopefully, that age is at least 5 and hopefully 10 years before you actually retire. This is the point where you should start mentally transitioning from the mindset of investing your retirement accounts for the purposes of growth into the attitude of structuring these accounts to maximize predictable income flows to last throughout your retired years.

When that time comes, you must fight the conventional wisdom that will attempt to keep you invested in areas such as stocks and bonds and start the diversification process into investment areas that will provide higher and more stable forms of income. Practical experience and history have taught us that relying on asset classes that can fluctuate in value can easily cause an otherwise well planned retirement to *run off the rails*.

In previous chapters we've discussed the 4% rule, whereby under normal circumstances, one can expect to withdraw 4% annual cash flow adjusted for inflation and expect a relatively high probability of not running out of money. First of all, 4% doesn't sound all that exciting, and if you follow it, it still doesn't mean market conditions won't derail you. Remember the Morningstar study mentioned in chapter 3 concluded a safe annual withdrawal rate to be 2.8%.

First of all, if you are fortunate enough to save $1 million in your retirement plans, you can withdraw a whopping $28,000 per year (adjusted for inflation) and be reasonably assured you won't outlive your money. I don't know about you, but I think that's terrible. That seems to be an excessive amount of risk and uncertainty to shoulder in order to receive such skimpy income. A large contingent of the financial services industry is bent on keeping you invested in stocks and bonds even though they admit that doing so will greatly restrict your access to enjoying the fruits of your lifelong savings.

Secondly, what if we have another 40% plus stock market correction such as the ones we suffered through in 2000-2003 and 2007-2009? How will the 4% rule hold up under those circumstances?

The answers are all around us. Just think about how many people you know who were forced to make drastic changes in their lifestyle because of those two market corrections? Many were forced to dramatically reduce their monthly budgets and subsequently their lifestyles and many rejoined the workforce.

Do you think I'm being far-fetched or an alarmist?

In April 2013, mutual fund elder statesman John Bogle, Senior Chairman and Founder of The Vanguard Group of mutual funds, stated in an interview aired on CNBC that he expects the stock market would have two (not one... but two) corrections of 30 to 50% over the next 10 years. To be fair, later in this interview, Bogle said he expects the markets to recover from these declines. The fact that Mr. Bogle, who has been a staunch defender of the stock market over his entire career, expects this type of volatility should tell us something. I applaud him for his frankness, but wonder if he's considered what corrections of this magnitude would do to the increasingly large percentage of the U.S. population preparing for retirement over that 10-year period?

As we discussed throughout this book, volatile assets and income don't mix.

Let's look at a simple example. Let's assume you save and invest diligently, and you grow a $1 million retirement account. Let's further assume. Therefore, in order to be prudent you set your income at $40,000 per year.

Now, one of those corrections that Mr. Bogle predicted occurs. The market and your retirement account fall 40%. After that, your $1 million account shrinks to $600,000. Furthermore, after you've taken out your $40,000 income that year, your account value ends up at $560,000.

In the next year, the same $40,000 income would result in a 7.14% distribution from your retirement account's reduced value ($40,000/$560,000). This, dear reader, has virtually no chance of being sustainable. The probability is you'll be forced to reduce your lifestyle and reduce the income taken from the retirement account in order to keep from running out of money.

In researching this section of the book, I could not find any documented research supporting the sustainability of income distributions from a portfolio comprised of stocks and bonds approaching a 7% level. The financial-academic community settled on the 4% rule as generally accepted because withdrawal rates that exceeded 4% resulted in increased probability of failure.

Therefore, it not only makes rational sense to reduce your exposure to volatile assets when retirement becomes more than a light at the end of the tunnel, but you've got the science of economics and finance to help guide you.

Unless you are in possession of a working crystal ball, future stock market corrections will be largely random, uncontrollable events. I suggest if you are 5 to 10 years from retirement, you should start the process of reducing exposure to volatile asset classes and replace them with stable asset classes designed to grow sustainable cash flows as discussed in Chapter 3.

I'm not advocating putting all your money in these riskless areas. But, if you're an individual who expects to use your retirement accounts as a future income source, I believe this to be justification for diversifying a large portion of your assets into these safer areas.

I understand that investing your money in guaranteed accounts is not as exciting as spreading it around the stock market, but it's *retirement* that should be exciting, not your retirement account.

Your Plan

Now that you spent the time to put together an IPS and investment plan, it's time to incorporate these into a retirement plan that might not work for anybody else on the planet. But it works for you.

First you need to establish your target.... how much income you'll need when you retire. This is profoundly more difficult than it sounds. The easiest way to do this is to determine your spending needs today and adjust them for changes that might occur in the future such as children becoming independent, paying off your mortgage or expenses only related to your job. There are other ways to arrive at your income target, but I have found this method helpful in working with my clients over the years.

Once you've determined your *income target,* you must assume a rate of inflation in order to properly discover the amount of income you'll likely need at your retirement date and throughout your retired years.

Income streams such as Social Security and pensions (if you're lucky enough to receive a pension) will most likely be partial solutions to your income target. Accurate estimates of these two income streams are very important. Contacting the Social Security Administration or going to ssa.gov can give you a relatively accurate reading of income to expect down the road. If you're expecting a pension, a quick inquiry to your HR department will most likely give you an amount that you can reasonably rely on for your retirement income estimates.

After you receive these figures, you must determine how you can maximize their efficiency. For example, Social Security benefits increase if you defer the start date. Full retirement age is typically around age 66, and every year you defer starting benefits income increases your benefits around 8% annually (until age 70). This can result in a few hundred thousand dollars of additional income over your lifetime.

Typically, company pensions will increase with additional years of service and salary increases. Whether you work for a private company or a government entity, pensions may be calculated differently; in order to maximize its income potential, it's important to understand how your pension works.

When calculating your income target, it's important to determine *if* your various forms of cash flow are adjusted for inflation. Fortunately Social Security has a cost-of-living increase or COLA built in, which helps repress inflation's effects. Pensions are another story. Most government pensions come with a COLA, but private pensions typically don't. To be safe, check with your HR department.

Once you've determined how much of a role Social Security and pensions will play in solving your income target, you can now go about solving for the gap. If you calculate you need $10,000 of monthly income at retirement and your pension and Social Security add up to $6,000 per month, your gap is $4,000. This is the figure that must come from other sources (typically your retirement accounts) in order to adequately fund your lifestyle throughout retirement.

Financial Handcuffs

The average American family spends roughly 34.5% of its monthly income on servicing personal debt. This debt may include mortgage payments, credit cards, automobiles and personal loans. As you can imagine, if over one-third of your income is already spoken for prior to receiving your paycheck or retirement check, you're effectively placing handcuffs around your lifestyle.

We discussed debt's pitfalls and ways to eliminate it in Chapter 3. I can't stress enough the importance of "debt reduction" as a part of your retirement plan. Debt not only siphons away income that can be used to fund your lifestyle, it also in most cases is tax inefficient. The money you're paying to various banks or finance companies is usually after-tax income. Payments for credit card debt, automobile loans and personal loans is currently not tax deductible, meaning that for each dollar you pay for these debts you must earn approximately $1.30, depending on your federal and state income tax bracket. Currently interest on mortgage debt for your personal home and even a vacation home is deductible; however, there continue to be rumblings from Washington regarding changes that may limit or possibly eliminate this deduction. It's a good idea to keep your ear close to the ground for possible changes.

You may be thinking: *Everyone seems to have it, so is debt really that bad?* The answer is... Yes.

Let me put it another way. If your monthly debt payments equal $3,000 (mortgage, credit card, automobile and personal loans), you'd need $720,000 earning 5% annually in order to produce $3,000 per month. Therefore, your debt would cost the equivalent of having a $720,000 investment producing spendable income.

Now, let me make it a bit worse. Let's assume that 50% of this $3,000 debt payment is for nondeductible items, meaning you must pay taxes on your income prior to paying your debts. Assuming you're in a 30% income tax bracket, your monthly debt payments would be equivalent to $828,000 earning 5% annually.

This plainly illustrates that controlling your debt can be equally as important as saving and investing your money, when it comes to generating income in order to support your lifestyle.

In Chapter 3, we put together a plan to reduce your debt by using the double-down approach starting with credit card, personal and automobile debt. This debt typically comes with higher interest rate charges along with being nondeductible, which should put first on your list to pay down before attacking deductible debt, such as your home.

Debt control is certainly a fundamental piece of a well-crafted retirement strategy. If you think about it logically, every dollar you don't spend on debt is a dollar you can spend *any way you want*.

Say No to the Tax Man

Similar to debt, taxes are a drag on your spendable income. While debt payments can be eliminated, taxes can't.

Not only should you employ tax advantaged strategies within your investment plan, such as the use of the tax-deferred and tax-free vehicles (Chapter 3), but you should make a deliberate effort to legally reduce your taxable income as much as possible.

Spend time with your financial advisor and tax consultant to determine which investment vehicles will provide a combination of growth and tax advantaged income. Not only should your tax planning include the optimum ways to save and invest your money, it should contain ideas to minimize your current taxable income. This means taking advantage of tax credits and deductions, as well as considering income shifting methods. For example, will contributing to a 401(k) reduce your taxable income enough to allow the use of the Hope tax credit for educational costs? Or, should you take your salary bonus this year, or push it into next year?

If these ideas seem foreign to you, you're probably paying too much in taxes.

The Federal Tax Code is currently almost 72,000 pages, and understanding how to best apply it to your individual circumstances can be challenging at best. Having a qualified tax advisor is essential to "long-term tax planning." Unfortunately, most of us use our tax preparers as a scorekeeper. We just visit them once a year with a handful of tax documents we've collected over the last 12 months and ask them to "take care of it."

For most people, there has been little planning except collecting all pertinent documents required by the IRS. If this sounds like you, you're most likely missing deductions or not considering strategies that may reduce your tax liability.

Instead of having the annual tax appointment with your tax preparer, consider incorporating an additional appointment for the purposes of tax planning. Establish an annual tax planning review. If they appear reluctant, unwilling or unsure, perhaps it's time to consider finding a new tax advisor. After all, if your tax advisor isn't willing to give you advice, you've just got a scorekeeper who's going to figure out how much money you owe the government every year. You need an individual who is willing to work directly with you to discuss and plan the best way for you to use the tax code to legally pay the least amount of tax.

Reducing the amount of tax liability will obviously provide you with additional funds to pay for your lifestyle and save for retirement. However, tax planning is an important subset of a well-designed retirement plan. Not only do you want to reduce tax liability today, but strategies should be put in place to reduce tax liability throughout retirement as well. Again, every dollar you save in taxes is a dollar you can spend any way you want.

Pass It On

This book's goal isn't to detail the various estate planning strategies, although they are an important piece of retirement plans. As we've mentioned numerous times, the goal of this book is income. You can't spend assets or net worth. You spend cash!

I suppose I could have devoted a chapter to the various estate planning strategies available, but a chapter would barely scratch the surface. Perhaps that's an idea for another book. It's safe to say that estate planning is not only important, but it's complicated and requires advice from a qualified professional.

Having said that, your retirement plan should consider who receives your money after you're done using it. Planning how your heirs inherit your assets can greatly increase the amount they receive and reduce the amount of taxes and transfer fees they'll pay.

There are various trusts that can be utilized to reduce or eliminate income and/or estate taxes upon your death. Which trusts are most applicable and best for your circumstances is a question for an estate planning attorney. Should you use a revocable or irrevocable trust? Should you start gifting your assets, how can you best avoid estate taxes, should you use income shifting methods, should you freeze the value of your estate, or should you put up walls between your assets and potential creditors? Trusts can be used to accomplish all of these concerns and more.

A trust is an arrangement that will be useful for some but not all of us. However, they should be considered for their potential advantages. Currently the estate tax threshold is $5,250,000 per person, meaning if you're married, $10,500,000 of your assets will be exempt from federal estate tax. The *American Taxpayer Relief Act*, signed in early 2013, made estates of $5 million per person adjusted for inflation exempt from federal estate taxes, permanent. I'm not sure what "permanent" means in Washington, but this current threshold makes estate taxes irrelevant for around 99% of the US population.

This does not render estate planning unnecessary. Issues like avoiding probate, transferring assets and powers of attorney are still concerns most of us should consider.

The basic estate planning ideas such as: *how your assets are titled and who are your beneficiaries are important to address.*

Should your assets be titled in your single name alone, joint tenancy or community property?

If you pass away with assets held in your name alone, these assets will be subject to probate even if you have a trust. A common misconception is that assets named in a "will" avoid probate...they don't.

Probate can be time consuming, expensive and completely avoidable with a bit of planning. If you are single, the use of revocable trusts, transfer on death (TOD) or pay on death (POD) arrangements can help you avoid the delays and costs of probate.

Accounts such as life insurance, annuities and all retirement accounts come with named beneficiaries. Upon your death, these assets will avoid probate and pass directly to your beneficiaries. It's important to understand that even if assets avoid probate, they still are valued for the purposes of estate taxes.

Joint tenant arrangements are a useful method to transfer ownership and avoid probate with married couples and business partners. There is an important distinction between "Joint Tenancy" and "Joint Tenancy with Rights of Survivorship." Over the years I've seen many mistakes made using these two types of titles. In most cases, "joint tenants" should be used when, at the death of one party, the intent is that their percentage ownership will transfer to someone other than the remaining joint tenant. In other words, if you and a friend purchase a building together as joint tenants, upon your death, you probably want your share of the asset to pass to your family, not your friend. Titling the building as joint tenants will accomplish this.

Because your percentage interest is considered to be inherited, your heirs will receive a 100% step-up in cost basis. Therefore, capital gains taxes can be greatly reduced if not eliminated on your share of the jointly held assets by using this arrangement.

On the other hand, if your intent is to pass your share to the remaining joint tenant at your death, Joint Tenants with Rights of Survivorship (JTROS) can achieve this. This is commonly used between married couples whose desire is to pass assets to the other at death. The step-up in tax basis differs with JTROS, with the surviving joint tenant receiving a step-up of 50% of the assets value as of the date of death.

Holding title as Community Property is only allowed through married couples. Although many states are considered to be "community property states," don't assume because you live in one that your marital assets are considered to be community property. Assets held as community property also avoid probate just as jointly held or JTROS can. However, community property has a distinct tax advantage over JTROS assets. Assets held as committee property receive a 100% step-up in basis upon death of either party, whereas JTROS effectively receive a 50% step-up.

Let's say 10 years ago, you and your spouse purchased a vacation home for $200,000 (tax basis), which is now worth $400,000. If you pass away, the $200,000 appreciation ($400,000-$200,000) will be taxed differently depending on its titling. If you held the title as JTROS you receive a step-up in basis on 50% of the gain or $100,000 making the cost basis $300,000. Therefore, if your surviving spouse sold the vacation home, they'd pay capital gains taxes on a $100,000 gain.

On the other hand, if the property was held as community property, at your death, your surviving spouse would receive a 100% step up in basis to $400,000, thereby alleviating capital gains taxes.

Because estate taxes differ in many states and tax considerations will vary depending upon your circumstances, it's important to contact a competent estate or tax advisor to determine what works best for you.

Beneficiary arrangements are another area of common misunderstanding. In many cases primary and contingent beneficiaries are selected without understanding potential pitfalls. It's not unusual to establish your beneficiaries using family members such as your spouse, children and grandchildren. If done properly, your assets will pass exactly as you desire. But commonly made assumptions can lead to unintended consequences.

Per Capita versus Per Stirpes

These terms are most probably unfamiliar to you and unfortunately they're alien to most stockbrokers and financial planners. Understanding these two concepts can help you avoid unwanted mistakes such as unintentionally disinherited members of your family.

These Latin terms are used to define how your assets are divided amongst your beneficiaries in the event that one or more of your beneficiaries predecease you.

Per Stirpes is a method of estate distribution whereby a surviving *branch* of the family receives an equal share. Per Capita is an alternative way of distribution, where heirs of the same generation will each receive an equal amount. The estate is divided into equal shares at the generation closest to the deceased, with surviving heirs.

Clear as mud, right......

Sometimes an example is the best way to describe competing concepts. Figures 20 and 21 display the difference between Per Stirpes and Per Capita.

In the Per Stirpes example in Figure 20, "A" specifies that their assets are to be divided among his beneficiaries in equal shares *per stirpes*. A has three children, B, C, and D. B has already passed, and left two children (grandchildren of A), B1 and B2. When A passes, under a distribution *per stirpes*, C and D will each receive one-third of the assets, and B1 and B2 each receive one-sixth. B1 and B2 make up one "branch" of the family, and together receive a one-third share.

If the Per Capita method is used, children C and D survive, so the assets are divided at their generation. There were three children, so each surviving child receives one-third. The remainder, B's share, is then divided in the same manner among B's surviving descendants. The result is the same as under Per Stirpes because B's one-third is distributed to B1 and B2 (one-sixth to each).

Now let's look at events that may cause unwanted consequences. In Figure 21, the *Per Capita and Per Stirpes* results would differ if D was also pre-deceased with one child, D1; under Per Stirpes, B1 and B2 would each receive one-sixth (half of B's one-third share), and D_1 would receive one-third (all of D's one-third share). Under Per Capita, the two-thirds remaining after C's one-third share was taken would be divided equally among all three children of B and D. Each would receive two-ninths: B_1, B_2, and D_1 would all receive two-ninths.

Figure 20

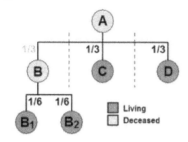

Figure 21

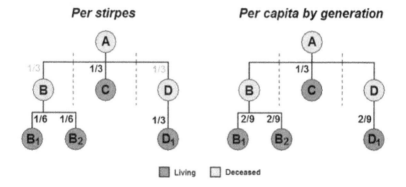

Are you scratching your head? The point I'm trying to make is a procedure as simple as naming your beneficiaries isn't really that simple. The outcome of making uninformed decisions may lead to unintended outcomes. Neither of these two methods takes into consideration the spouses of your children (sons and daughters-in-law). The spouses of your children would not be considered as part of the family branch and would be bypassed. In example 21, if B and D both had spouses as well as children, A's assets would bypass their spouses and go directly to the children. This may or may not be your intent, which shows that careful thought must go into the different scenarios and how they may affect the various members of your family.

When it comes to your family and their well-being, a little extra homework can avoid misunderstandings and potential squabbles.

What are you waiting for?

"Only put off until tomorrow what you are willing to die having left undone"

— Pablo Picasso

Throughout this book I tried to stress that consistent and sustainable income is King. Many times you have to look beyond the obvious and fight conventional wisdom in order to put together a retirement income plan that works for you. It's neither impossible nor unattainable; each of us can use various methods available to us to put together a plan that will supply the income that will feed our lifestyles throughout retirement.

So, if you've already got a written retirement plan or you're one of those who has one swirling around in your head, use this book as a guide to turn that plan into a blueprint for income that will take care of you and your family for the rest of your life.

Gather all the necessary data, such as existing investment and retirement plan statements, Social Security and pension income projections, debt and expense information. Then make a pot of coffee, get a sharp pencil and a calculator and start in.

Once you've figured out how much income you'll need, you can start putting together the income streams you'll have at retirement, such as Social Security and pension income. When you discover that these sources of income will probably not be enough to keep up with inflation and maintain your lifestyle, you can start looking at the methods and concepts discussed in this book. They'll help you to effectively and efficiently use the money you've accumulated through your savings, investment and retirement accounts to successfully fill that income gap.

Remember, you can't spend assets or net worth; you do, however, spend cash. Putting together your plan to produce predictable, sustainable retirement income isn't luck or happenstance. It takes careful consideration, hard work and persistence. In other words, it takes a plan.

"A plan without action is a dream, and action without a plan is a nightmare."

–Chinese Proverb